ACTING OUT: THE WORKBOOK

ACTING OUT: THE WORKBOOK

A Guide to the Development and Presentation of Issue-oriented, Audience-interactive, Improvisational Theatre

Mario Cossa, MA, RDT, CP
Sally S. Fleischmann Ember, Ed. D.
Lauren Grover
Jennifer L. Hazelwood, AS

ACCELERATED DEVELOPMENT
A member of the Taylor & Francis Group

USA	Publishing Office:	ACCELERATED DEVELOPMENT
		A member of the Taylor & Francis Group
		1101 Vermont Avenue, N.W., Suite 200
		Washington, DC 20005-3521
		Tel: (202) 289-2174
		Fax: (202) 289-3665
	Distribution Center:	ACCELERATED DEVELOPMENT
		A member of the Taylor & Francis Group
		1900 Frost Road, Suite 101
		Bristol, PA 19007-1598
		Tel: (215) 785-5800
		Fax: (215) 785-5515
UK		Taylor & Francis Ltd.
		1 Gunpowder Square
		London EC4A 3DE UK
		Tel: 0171 583 0490
		Fax: 0171 583 0581

ACTING OUT: The Workbook—A Guide to the Development and Presentation of Issue-oriented, Audience-interactive, Improvisational Theatre

1 2 3 4 5 6 7 8 9 0   BRBR   9 8 7 6

This book was set in Times Roman by Monotype Composition, Inc. The editor was Judith L. Aymond. Technical development by Cynthia Long. Cover design by Michelle Fleitz. Printing and binding by Braun-Brumfield, Inc.

A CIP catalog record for this book is available from the British Library.
∞ The paper in this publication meets the requirements of the ANSI Standard Z39.48-1984 (Permanence of Paper)

Library of Congress Cataloging-in-Publication Data

Acting out: the workbook: a guide to the development and presentation of issue-oriented, audience-interactive, improvisational theatre / Mario Cossa . . . [et al.].
    p. cm.
    Includes bibliographical references.

    1. Psychodrama.   2. Group psychotherapy for teenagers.   3. Theater and youth.
4. Drama in education.   I. Cossa, Mario.
RJ505.P89A73   1996
616.89′1523—dc20

96-15842
CIP

ISBN 1-56032-534-8

TABLE OF CONTENTS

PART B
ISSUE-ORIENTED SCENARIOS

PART C
GENERAL REFERENCES AND RESOURCES

ACKNOWLEDGEMENTS

This workbook represents the efforts of all the members, staff, interns, audiences, support people, and agencies who have contributed to the first seven years of the ACTING OUT Program. Special commendations are due to the actors or members of ACTING OUT, two of whom are coauthors, whose spontaneity and enthusiasm for improvisation led to the creation of many of the scenarios and variations contained in this workbook, and to Tricia Mettler, our 1992–1993 program year intern from Antioch-New England Graduate School.

We at ACTING OUT are grateful as well to Monadnock Substance Abuse Services, which has been our program's sponsoring agency since 1991. The support of its staff, administration, and Board have been much appreciated. In 1995, our agency and our program became part of Monadnock Family Services, a Community Mental Health provider.

The development of these materials was funded, in part, by a Drug-free Schools and Communities Program Grant awarded to ACTING OUT for September 1992 through September 1993.

ACTING OUT also would like to acknowledge our other major funding sources: the New Hampshire Bureau of Substance Abuse Services, the Monadnock United Way, the State of New Hampshire Department of Education (Peer Theater for HIV Prevention Program), the Cheshire County Commissioners, the Marshall Frankel Foundation, the Dorothy Jordan Chadwick Fund, and the

A. Erland and Hazel N. Goyette Memorial Fund within the New Hampshire Charitable Foundation.

Many thanks to all.

Mario Cossa, MA, RDT, CP, ACTING OUT Program Director
Sally S. Fleischmann Ember, M.Ed., ACTING OUT Educational Coordinator
Lauren Grover
Jennifer L. Hazelwood, AS
June, 1996

PART A
BASIC INFORMATION

In Part A are four chapters that contain basic information for the ACTING OUT program. These four chapters need to be studied and understood fully before doing any scenework.

Chapter 1 provides purposes and benefits and how to use most effectively the procedures identified in this workbook.

In Chapter 2 are limitations and cautions that must be considered. The leader is to understand his or her own qualifications and capability for working with ACTING OUT scenes and scenarios, since these can bring forth a release of emotional energy.

Chapter 3 raises items to be considered about leaders and participants.

Chapter 4 contains the specifics for activities to be associated with scenes and respective scenarios. Also provided are some things to do and some things to avoid. Details for establishing a program using these activities conclude this section.

IMPROVISATION AND ACTING OUT

ACTING OUT (AO) is a program for teens that was introduced to the Monadnock Region of Southwestern New Hampshire in the Fall of 1989. AO combines expressive arts group therapy with training and performance opportunities in improvisational theatre.

Although the main focus of the program is on the needs of its members, AO's public side—as an issue-oriented, audience-interactive, improvisational theatre company—has enjoyed an enthusiastic reception in New England. It is this particular aspect of AO, of using improvisation to explore contemporary issues, that we have endeavored to share in this workbook.

When the workbook was first conceived, a subtitle of "We Are Not Children and We Do Not Do Skits" was considered. This statement was made by a member in response to an introduction of one AO group at a state educators' convention. The host had said, "The children are now going to do some skits for you," and the group's actors were righteously indignant. These actors, who routinely handled issues including date rape, suicide, HIV infection, and many other sensitive topics, certainly had earned the right to be addressed as young men and women; the impact of the process that they shared went far beyond what one usually would expect from a "skit."

PURPOSES AND BENEFITS OF THIS WORKBOOK

Teachers, guidance counselors, residential treatment therapeutic staff, therapists, youth group leaders, and all who work with upper-elementary, middle school, high school, and older adolescents could find techniques and activities within this workbook for use with members of most groups. Therefore, this workbook is intended to serve these types of youth leaders and educators.

Audience-interactive theatre has the power to engage viewers and participants and actors on many levels. The AO procedures quickly move out of the cognitive realm, of merely what we *think* about an issue, into the realm of feelings. On this level is where changes in attitudes and behaviors can best or most often be stimulated. As authors, we are eager and excited to share this process with you and your groups of young people by showing you how to utilize the process in your own groups.

Although the focus of this workbook is not to explore in detail the counseling and therapeutic components of AO, it is important to recognize that AO in its current form is partly a theatre program, partly a counseling program. In the last two sections of this chapter, some general applications of these techniques and activities to therapeutic and educational settings are discussed.

It is possible, and even necessary, for educators and leaders without clinical training to learn these techniques for and solely to utilize the theatrical component; offering ideas for how to do that is a major purpose of this workbook. For more information about combining both components and about the qualifications of leaders, please refer to Chapter 3, Leader and Participant Information. If more information is needed, please contact the AO staff (ACTING OUT, P. O. Box 196, Keene, NH 03431, 603-357-5882).

In later sections, benefits are detailed for all participants, including observers. In this section, discussing purposes seems most useful. Generally, using drama and theatrical techniques or activities in classrooms enhances and augments more traditional approaches. Teachers unfamiliar with using multiarts often can begin with role-plays without needing additional training. Many books exist that offer inexperienced leaders ideas and suggestions for facilitating role-plays.

This workbook is designed to encourage those who are ready to go beyond simple role-plays to do so, whether in classrooms or more clinical settings. Our experiences, and experiences of others in these fields, have shown that young people, particularly adolescents, benefit greatly from chances to experiment in a fantasy world or alternative reality, rather than the "real world," with drugs, decisions about sex, violence, harassment, family conflicts, and school conflicts. Scenarios included in this workbook have been designed by young people who have used them and refined them through their use, so these scenes have been "proven" to be effective.

Appropriate leadership combined with these activities definitely will evoke deeper and more insightful discussions on almost any topic the group explores. These discussions often can lead to more thoughtful and informed decision-making, a stronger internal locus-of-control, broader understandings of the *other* side(s), and greater communication skills even for observers, and assuredly for actors or performers.

If your goals include building and developing these skills, this workbook will offer ways to do so with your group(s). If you just want to increase your members' theatre skills, or add "fun" elements to group time, enjoy these activities, for they will accomplish those goals as well.

FORMAT OF THIS WORKBOOK

Part A (Chapters 1 through 4) explores the techniques, philosophies, and foundations of doing this type of theatre with teens in classroom or group settings and in public performances. Part B (Chapters 5 through 12) offers several scenarios for each of eight issue categories, with specific resources for each category as well as information about timing, frequency repetition, and post-scenework processing. Part C lists general professional resources and references.

ABOUT GENDER-INCLUSIVE LANGUAGE

As a program concerned with equity and justice as well as personal growth and development, consistent efforts must be made to be inclusive of all social and cultural groups. In this workbook, "he or she" or other gender-inclusive double terminology has been used, except where the gender of a character is relevant (e.g., in the case of a pregnant teen). Leaders need to remember that, in theatrical scenework, gender roles may be reversed, doubled, stereotyped, or exaggerated to make a point.

CURRICULA AND ACTION METHODS

Social science, language arts, speech, drama, citizenship, health education, and many interdisciplinary courses could be enhanced greatly by utilizing improvisation and the subsequent discussions to develop a variety of communication and information skills. Many schools currently offer integrated curriculum days, weeks, or even years, based upon a theme. Scenarios listed in this workbook are prototypes for thematic categories of any kind that can be developed into scenework for classroom use. Guidance counselors also can utilize these techniques and activities to augment the particular curriculum requirements for each age group.

Younger children could create scenes to explore history, social issues, government, and/or current events; older students could expand upon these to include personal experiences. Student-directed research could precede developing the scenes used in all age groups.

If a school is offering assemblies for a particular theme or curricula sharing, small groups of experienced improvisers could prepare some potential scenes for audience interaction; alternatively, improvised scenework could become scripted (partially or completely) and used as a theatrical performance.

CLINICAL APPLICATIONS AND TREATMENT PLANS

Using these techniques and activities in clinical settings is recommended only if the leaders are trained in action methods (e.g., role-play, role-training, psychodrama, sociodrama, drama therapy, etc.). Within the types of populations often served in clinical settings, the group members could move quickly into intense affect and would need adequate therapeutic leadership to contain and guide the scenework and post-scenework processing.

The recommendation is that the scenarios remain in the sociodramatic modality rather than in individually-centered scenework unless these activities are used as a warm-up for protagonist-centered psychodramatic work led by a trained psychodramatist. In other words, leaders should be aware of goals for using sociodramatic versus psychodramatic approaches, and this factor will be dependent upon one's client population, intentions, and treatment plans. If you, the reader or leader, are unfamiliar with many of these action methods, the recommendation is that you use these themes and suggested scenes to work with the respective issues in general rather than to re-create or work in-depth with any individual group member's actual issues.

Differences between uses of these activities within clinical settings and educational settings are largely differences of intent. But the clinical setting is also different in its expectations of group therapy time and therapy's impact on participants. Strong leadership is recommended in both settings, as will be discussed in Chapter 3.

With this in mind, several client populations are well-served by utilization of AO techniques and activities and are as follows:

those with eating disorders,
recovering substance abusers,
sexual and/or physical abuse survivors,
those in violent and/or abusive relationships, and
those with school or family problems.

Basically, any group that has members who can communicate sufficiently and that has some members who are willing to be performers could use these activities.

Chapter 2

LIMITATIONS AND CAUTIONS

In Chapter 3, some limitations exist regarding criteria for appropriate leaders or teachers and participants. Please refer to Chapter 3 before beginning your own program or using these scenarios. In addition, experience has shown that there are other cautions worth mentioning before proceeding.

Sufficient time is needed to warm up, to discuss and choose from which scenarios to create improvisational scenes, to create the scenes, and to process the scenework afterwards. If limited time is available or if the group meets infrequently, careful choices must be made as to which activities the group should do for each meeting. Some processing time should occur in each meeting as well as some "cool down" time, since some role-plays, scenes, and subsequent processing can get very intense. Some of the Warm-up Activities provided in Chapter 4, or other similar games, also may be useful just before closing.

Leaders or teachers should read Chapters 1 through 4 and scan several scenarios before beginning to use any of the activities. This familiarity and information is vital to professional responsibility. Likewise, if sections of this workbook are shared with other leaders, those who have not read Chapters 1 through 4 will be severely disadvantaged, and perhaps their groups or classes could be harmed. Extending a helping hand and utilizing techniques that enable persons to introspect and explore with others require a professional person skillful with professional procedures. The scenarios can be fun, rewarding, and interesting activities, but they also can evoke deep, intense feelings and issues that leaders must be prepared to handle effectively within their groups.

With limited budgets and the proliferation of photocopying and fax machines, professionals may be tempted just to give verbal support and explanations along with a few pages of this workbook to a new leader. PLEASE DO NOT DO THIS! The reason is far more important than trying to sell workbooks. The authors truly believe in the value of these background materials. We do not judge it to be safe or professional just to read a few parts and then begin scenework with any group unless the leaders are skilled and experienced socio- or psychodramatists with theatre training.

We wish for you rewarding experiences in your endeavors. Feedback on your successes as well as difficulties in using this material would be greatly appreciated. Address correspondence to ACTING OUT, P. O. BOX 196, Keene, NH 03431, or telephone 603-357-5882.

Chapter 3

LEADER AND PARTICIPANT INFORMATION

This workbook is intended for a wide range of users; therefore, a clear and complete framework has been provided so that teachers and group leaders with no prior experience in theatre and limited clinical experience can make excellent use of this process. Some groups may choose to use this material as an aid to discussion, for exploration of issues that they may be considering in their class or group. For those leaders whose groups are utilizing theatre as an educational or motivational tool already, methods and suggestions in this workbook will support their growth in both the scope and range of their work.

QUALIFICATIONS FOR LEADERS

For leaders who do not have a strong background in improvisational theatre, but who wish to start a similar group or program, this workbook offers a foundation. It is not intended, however, to be a beginner's manual in how to do improvisational theatre. Other excellent works are available to supplement training and experience in this area. Some are listed in Part C, General References and Resources.

As mentioned in Chapter 1, if AO is used in clinical settings, leaders must be prepared with training in action methods in order to guide professionally as well as "go with the group" when the desired effects are achieved. The added benefits of clinical use are the following: time can be used in group therapy to process these issues; additional group time may be scheduled to do improvisation and post-scenework processing; and further group time may be available for follow-up, especially in a residential setting.

Strong leaders or teachers are required for this processing in groups, because the energy levels and emotional triggering can become high or intense. Teachers and leaders with calm, directive styles, strong senses of humor, and the ability and willingness to be flexible and to change directions instantaneously are ideal. Low levels of fear and or distaste about confrontation, conflict, intensity, and witnessing pain are also useful, because many of the improvisations can elicit scenes in which any or all of these can occur for both participants and observers. The subsequent discussions can be emotional as well. A newer leader with the desire and potential to develop these characteristics could work with a more experienced, stronger leader and quickly gain in all of these areas, as ACTING OUT internship programs with graduate students have shown.

CRITERIA FOR SELECTION OF PARTICIPANTS

Educational Groups

Since mainstreaming occurs in most classrooms in the 1990s, the mixture of abilities, language proficiencies, emotional and mental stabilities, physical abilities, and the class size may restrict groups from using some of these scenarios, but using the techniques, especially Warm-up Activities (see Chapter 4), works well in any group. Ideally, groups in which many students have special needs or need extra help to participate would have additional adults or older participants to translate, assist in other ways, and monitor along with the primary leader or teacher, particularly in large or extremely diverse groups. If only one leader or teacher is available, beginning slowly, constantly monitoring participation, offering low-stakes activities (e.g., students could "pass" or observe before participating), or offering multiple levels of involvement would make single leader groups more possible. However, single leader groups in which intense issues are addressed, even when many students are willing and able to participate, are not ideal.

Clinical Groups

As stated earlier, most young people who can participate in group therapy would be eligible to participate in a program using these techniques. Awareness should be exercised in doing this kind of work with young people with dissociative disorders, however, as role-playing can trigger dissociation. Choices made by leaders, based upon leaders' previous training, experiences, and personal characteristics, should determine to what extent and into what types of materials groups venture for each scenario. For more information about how to work responsibly and intensively with young people, contact ACTING OUT (P. O. Box 196, Keene, NH 03431, 603-357-5882).

All Groups

Many groups do not select participants, and many groups have mandatory attendance. The ACTING OUT program works best with volunteers, but involving students and clients in these activities with appropriate leadership can create stronger interpersonal connections within the groups and between the members and the leaders, regardless of the origins of the group. Based on experience with several different groups, the recommendation is to allow members or participants to choose their own levels of participation as each activity allows; this increases feelings of safety and respect among members.

Members are encouraged to take risks, with support and validation, by setting ground rules (norms) within the group before beginning scenework. A good procedure is to use a norm-creating activity in one of the group's first sessions or classes and then to reinforce the agreed-upon norms at each meeting. Some of these are discussed in Chapter 4. The norms most often helpful are confidentiality, mutual respect, punctuality, sobriety, and nonviolence. These are pacts that members make together that create an atmosphere in which serious issues can be addressed safely. It is necessary, therefore, to have options for removing members, either temporarily or permanently, who do not or cannot adhere to group norms, or at least for relegating those members to observer roles during some activities.

Chapter 4

HOW TO USE THIS WORKBOOK

The chapters of this workbook are organized according to background topics (Part A, Basic Information, Chapters 1 through 4), issues (Part B, Issue-oriented Scenarios, Chapters 5 through 12), and resources (Part C, General References and Resources).

FORMAT AND USES OF ISSUES AND SCENARIOS

Within each issue category are a number of scenario outlines. Most of these scenarios have been presented, in one form or another and at one time or another, by ACTING OUT members in various presentations to a wide range of audiences. Whether you plan to use them solely within your classroom or group or to develop pieces for public presentation, you will need to provide supportive starting points. Once you have begun, you probably will start creating scenarios of your own that incorporate the specific interests and capacities of your group.

Each scenario chapter includes material that is appropriate at various age levels; some material is clearly appropriate across grade levels. Some material may require modification to serve the needs of younger or older participants. Some material is more limited. The needs and abilities of your group and its audience will determine which scenarios will be useful to you.

Each page of Part B of the workbook is devoted to a specific scenario. Chapters 1 through 4 discuss in detail how to use each scenario and the philosophies behind the ACTING OUT format.

BASIC SCENARIO CONSIDERATIONS

For each scenario, you are provided with five basic considerations: Who, What, Where, What Would Happen If . . ., and Things to Think About.

Who

This is a list of how many people are needed in a scene, their ages, their relationships to one another, and relevant background material. Names are used only to distinguish characters of the same general type, such as a group of parents or people at a party.

You are encouraged to have your group "flesh out" the descriptions offered before beginning to work on a scene. You might even try the same situations using different characters.

ACTING OUT members usually use their own names to avoid confusion. ACTING OUT members always use a disclaimer (see the Working with Who, What, and Where section of this chapter) to clarify for actors and audiences that the characters and their reactions to the situations that they portray are not necessarily related to the actors' own personalities, life situations, or beliefs.

What

This is the actual content of the scene, and each actor should approach it in terms of his or her WHO. This section can be modified, of course, to meet the specific needs of your group and its experiences with the issues presented.

Where

This is the suggested location in which the scene takes place. Feel free to experiment with this or other locations.

What Would Happen If . . .

This is a list of questions that suggests variations on the WHO, WHAT, and WHERE that you might want to try out.

Things to Think About

This is a list of questions whose answers are important to explore while working on the scene. The information then might be worked into the scene, depending on whether your group members are learning for themselves, sharing information with others, or both. Identifying resources in your community that can respond to your questions is an important part of this process. New information becomes available almost daily in many of these topic areas, and your group will want and need to know it.

WORKING WITH WHO, WHAT, AND WHERE

Three basic elements are needed for an improvisational scene or role-play: WHO, WHAT and WHERE. For more detailed exercises in developing these concepts, see Spolin (1975, 1985a, 1985b). If your group is not aiming to develop pieces for public performance, the following brief descriptions will suffice.

Basic Elements

In creating scenes, ACTING OUT members work with a disclaimer. It states: *"Even though we may use our own names in the scenes we do, the opinions expressed and the experiences represented by our characters are not necessarily our own."* This disclaimer is important whether or not the material is being presented publicly. It frees each actor to experiment with new ways of behaving without fear of being judged personally for choices made by the character.

ACTING OUT groups work with scenes utilizing Spolin's (1975, 1985a, 1985b) format of presenting the WHO, WHAT, and WHERE elements of each scene as a set of questions to be answered and explored by the actors and members of the group. In the scenarios offered in this workbook, WHO, WHAT, and WHERE are provided. Some variations that can be explored also are offered. Groups are encouraged to expand on the information given to develop variations on the original scene.

> **WHO:** Who are the characters in the scene? What are their names, ages, and relationship to each other? The actors, with audience support, should develop a brief history for the characters and their previous interactions.

WHAT: What is the issue being explored in the scene? What is the major concern of each character? What does each character hope to gain from the interaction? (More about this aspect is discussed in the following section, "The Importance of V.O.T.E.") In defining the WHAT, actors are encouraged *not* to plan what they will say and do in advance but to be certain *what* the scene is about. Actors and audience may come to the realization during the role-play that underlying issues exist that were not stated at the outset. If this is the case, the scene can be reenacted to reflect these underlying issues.

WHERE: Where is the scene taking place? By defining the WHERE in detail, using chairs or desks to represent various objects in the WHERE, an environment can be created, which helps actors interact spontaneously and naturally. If the scene moves beyond "just talking" and engages in action (e.g., eating breakfast, packing a suitcase, or getting ready for a party), it becomes more interesting to watch. At the same time, if the actors focus their attention on interacting in the WHERE, the dialogue emerges more spontaneously.

THE IMPORTANCE OF V.O.T.E.

Taking Improvisation to a Deeper Level

As the improvisational actors become more comfortable in their work, you can introduce a format for examining their scenes that is represented by the acronym V.O.T.E. Not only does this examination provide another level of depth to the acting, but it also gives actors practice in using improvisation to explore personal choices and behaviors. V.O.T.E. is explained below.

V is for VICTORY: What does the character really want? Sometimes another way to address this question is through discussion of "motivation." The term VICTORY is preferred because it implies higher stakes. One has to *strive* to achieve a VICTORY. A VICTORY statement always should be reduced to a simple, declarative sentence: "I want him or her to like me"; "I want to get my own way"; or "I want to be treated like an adult."

O is for OBSTACLE: What stands in the way of the character's VICTORY? The obstacle may be internal ("I'm afraid to try"), or external ("My mother won't let me"). Sometimes one character's VICTORY becomes another's OBSTACLE. Sometimes the apparent OBSTACLE is only a mask for something the character is trying to avoid facing.

T is for TACTICS: What can the character do to overcome the OBSTACLE? This is the foundation for a number of possible variations on the same scene. As actors explore TACTICS, they begin to discover the relationships between behaviors and consequences.

E is for EMOTIONS: What feelings are stimulated by the characters' quests to employ various TACTICS to overcome their OBSTACLES and achieve their VICTORIES? Careful exploration of EMOTIONS can reveal that often one feeling (e.g., anger) may mask deeper feelings (e.g., hurt, fear, grief, etc.).

In using the V.O.T.E. format in ACTING OUT work, what has been discovered is that members begin to apply it to their personal issues as well. This is a prime example of the way in which role-playing theatre training can serve as life training.

Note: ACTING OUT Director, Mario Cossa, was first introduced to the V.O.T.E. system by Al Corona, a director and theatre instructor from Boston, MA. Corona credited the system to Robert Cohen from Irvine, CA.

SOME THOUGHTS ON AUDIENCE-INTERACTIVE THEATRE

When actors and viewers co-create a scene, theatre becomes an active exploration of issues. Whether in a performance or classroom setting, the same principles apply. Many ways exist to involve the audience, who may be observers within the group or class or an actual audience of "outsiders."

Setting Up the Scene

Viewers can offer the actors suggestions for rounding out characters' personal histories. (What if a character who is concerned about his or her friend's cigarette smoking has lost a family member recently due to lung cancer?) They can offer variations on the WHAT. (What if a suicidal friend is holding a bottle of sleeping pills?) They may make suggestions on the WHERE as well. (What if the principal has a habit of patrolling this section of the school yard?)

Questioning and Giving Advice

From time to time, the scene can be "frozen" so that the viewers can ask the characters questions about why they are doing or saying certain things. Viewers also might give advice as to how to handle a situation.

Angel, Devil, and Other Inner Voices

In exploring issue-oriented theatre, characters reach *choice points* in which the decision of the moment will affect the outcome of the scene. The inner-thought process that the character is undergoing can be concretized by having additional actors come into the playing area and take on the angel and devil voices within, such as often is presented in cartoons. This provides another opportunity for audience interaction as well as a chance to clarify this choice and all the considerations that might be part of it. Inner-voice characters also can be used effectively in scenes to represent what characters may be thinking but are not saying. In both of these instances, the actor playing the particular character could voice these thoughts in "asides" to the viewers, but frequently the use of additional actors creates more interest and insight.

Making Decisions

Whenever a major decision must be made, whether or not the inner voices have been heard, an excellent technique is to involve the audience in the decision. It is a great way to generate discussion within the group and to maintain the interest level of those not on stage. When the group is divided on the decision that should be made, several possibilities can be played out to discover what the likely consequences of each might be. It is generally a good idea to be able to explore consequences as well as choices. Sometimes this may lead into another scene, such as with a youth who, having chosen to drink with friends, is later confronted by a parent at home. Viewers also may suggest possible variations on the way the scene is evolving by offering different characters, plot twists, choices, and so forth.

Not Physicalizing Aggression

Although audiences often will suggest a fight between characters, we believe that this type of behavior is not to be condoned and that the purposes of ACTING

OUT are not fulfilled by adding physicalized aggression to the already abundant opportunities young people have to view acts of violence. If a physical altercation is essential to move a scene along, it is important for the actors to mime the interaction as briefly as possible, with a minimum of physical contact. Even in scenes about abuse, the purpose is to present the effects of the abuse and not to recreate the abuse for the audience.

Using Comedy

When ACTING OUT initially was created, we were so focused on the seriousness of topics that, although presentations were never dull, they were often heavy and depressing. We have come to believe that comic moments, even in the most serious scenes, actually can help the audience integrate the material presented. In presentations to school audiences, a balance of serious and lighter material has been found to work best. Parents and teachers who have seen ACTING OUT as it developed over time have commented that this balance is much more effective than our previous one. The director or group leader should set limits so that scenes do not degenerate into silliness or ridicule of the material or character types presented.

Benefits

As seen above, many opportunities exist for all persons present to be involved in ways that engage the young people (and the adults) on many levels. Countless times after performances, audience members who did not participate have approached a participant or leader of the troupe to show thanks, to demonstrate a new insight, to show new thinking or questioning, or to share the tears or laughter that the scenes evoked. Guidance counselors and teachers in schools in which AO has performed have telephoned AO staff members days, weeks, even months later to discuss the continuing impact of given performances and post-scenework processing discussions. Community groups, after only one performance, often increase their members' awarenesses of the issues raised in the AO scenes. This often translates into better-funded and more diverse programming for young people in these communities.

On a smaller scale, in every ACTING OUT group meeting, each member frequently states his or her feelings after each scenario, whether having been in a performing or observing role. What will become clear from these statements is that being in either role benefits members through the same routes mentioned above and also through enhanced intragroup bonding.

SELF-DISCLOSURE AND CONFIDENTIALITY

Working Responsibly with a Powerful Medium

Theatre is a powerful medium for evoking feelings and eliciting personal disclosures in participants—actors and audience members alike. When working with sensitive issues, it is not at all uncommon for actors in rehearsal or audience members in performance either to share spontaneously that they have experienced a similar kind of situation in their lives or to express emotions. This is the reason that appropriate leadership is essential (see Chapters 2 and 3).

Assure Confidentiality.   Teachers, counselors, therapists, and other leaders working in this medium must state expectations about confidentiality clearly. Any personal material that is disclosed by group members is not to be shared publicly. An important procedure is to make sure that each person clearly understands and accepts these limits and the extent to which confidentiality is to be maintained. Legal requirements for the reporting of abuse and intentions to harm self or others should be stated clearly. Group leaders must know what their responsibilities are in these matters, and they must be aware of the appropriate resources and support services available if reporting is required or social services are needed.

Nondisclosure.   Also, actors and leaders must understand the policy about not sharing personal material with the audience. That is the reason why performers need to use the disclaimer: "Although we may use our own names in our scenes, the ideas expressed and the experiences we represent are not necessarily our own." (See earlier section of this chapter, Working with Who, What, and Where.)

Control Depth of Scene.   Formats and restrictions similar to those presented here need to be followed, even when performing just for participants acting within the scenario. This is especially so when leaders, such as teachers in educational settings, are not trained in action method psychotherapies. Keeping the scenes general allows issues to be addressed without directly involving anyone's personal material. Containment is important because of time limitations, leader inexperience, and the need to create safety for the group, so plan the use of meeting time thoughtfully.

Identify and Discuss Resources.   When doing presentations for audiences on sensitive topics, such as abuse of any kind, suicide, or alcoholism, a good procedure is to inform audience members and adult leaders about the appropriate resources for dealing with these issues if personal memories and feelings are evoked by the presentation. A vital part of the AO process is to talk about these issues and to do so responsibly.

Role of the Leader and Professional Boundaries

Many questions arise during group meetings about which activities leaders ought to participate in and to what extent. In classroom settings, teachers have more relaxed professional boundaries than leaders in most clinical settings have, but experiences with AO techniques have created some recommendations:

1. Leaders ought to participate at their own discretion and based upon their abilities, in all physical activities or warm-ups, opening and closing circle-types of activities, and any other low-stakes, nonrevealing activities.
2. Leaders should not participate, except as facilitators or guides, in the creation of and initial parts of scenarios, since leaders will be needed to guide/direct the scenework. Experienced leaders, with experienced groups, may bend these rules a bit, especially if a participant is needed and no one else volunteers. But, on-stage directing is difficult, and often confusing, and should be done by experienced leaders only.

    Another strongly-made suggestion is to keep the leaders' and participants' roles separated by age: If young people play their own or similar ages, leaders play adults; if young people play adults, leaders then may play young people. This avoids role-playing that can confuse boundaries, such as having leaders and participants involved as peers in scenework about dating.
3. When issues arise in which members are revealing personal material, either during discussions or scenework, leaders may choose how much to reveal about themselves, depending upon the circumstances, of course. It is one thing, however, to state simply, "I also have experienced [blank], and I know a little bit about how that feels," and quite another to use group time for a leader's therapy. Even telling the story may be too much for members to handle from a leader. Please be aware of the difference: This time is for participants, not leaders. If you find you need additional support, please obtain it during your off hours.
4. Many leaders or teachers discover information about their own childhoods and adolescences through leading or participating in this type of scenework, especially if the scenework becomes a full psychodramatic scene. The evocative nature of this work demands that leaders take good care of themselves. Supervision is often insufficient to meet this need. If appropriate self-care means joining your own group for therapy or

support, or going into individual therapy, please consider it time well spent in service to yourself and your group(s).

EVALUATING

Evaluating within an Educational Setting

Tests, exams, quizzes, portfolios, grades—these do not seem congruent with the principles and purposes of the activities presented here. Yet schools usually must conform to these types of evaluative instruments, and teachers must comply. A few suggestions are offered:

1. Make attendance and conforming to the group norms the only criteria for grading.
2. Have students grade themselves, based upon goals they set for themselves at the onset of the program or unit.
3. Either have writing in a journal be a part of every post-scenework processing time or assign that writing for homework. Make length rather than content requirements the evaluative measure so that criteria for assessment are based upon compliance (or efforts toward compliance) with numbers of pages or lines written rather than the nature of what is written, as long as the topics are addressed.

   Collect these journals weekly (having made it clear that you will do this), and dialogue with each student about his or her insights, feelings, questions, and comments. In large classes with only one teacher or leader, collect journals from each student every other week or every third week, dividing the class into subgroups for this and perhaps for other purposes. Home groups such as this can be effective for scenario-creating as well as post-scenework processing, because groups larger than 10 to 12 usually silence some members because of time limitations or other restrictions on participation.
4. Make these activities a part of each unit or quarter or semester, and have participation constitute a fraction of each total grade earned. Use one of the above measures to determine the grade earned.
5. Meet with guidance counselors, special education teachers, or both (if you are not one yourself) and discover if any of your students' Individual Educational Plan (IEP) goals may be met through these activities, an accompanying journal, or both. Let students know if this is possible.
6. Meet with English as a Second Language (ESL) teachers (if you are not one) to find out how to enhance limited English speakers' participa-

tion, and to invite the ESL teachers' insights and advice as to the scenarios that would be most useful during certain parts of ESL students' English language development.

Evaluating within a Therapeutic Setting

ACTING OUT was developed in both a clinical and an educational setting, so the authors are aware of aspects of evaluation in both areas. For the clinical setting, the suggestion is to establish Personal Growth Plans (PGPs) with each member each year. The form should have a section for the participant to mark issues or qualities that are strengths, that are challenges, and that are of primary importance to the member at that time. Then, members write personal goals and ideas of how to utilize the group to gain support for achieving those goals during that year. These goals are shared with the group and reviewed periodically. Time in final group meetings is used to provide self-evaluative data as well as to offer group feedback to each member, using these PGPs and stated goals as the foundations.

Leaders often are helped through keeping limited but weekly notes about each member's participation, issues, and scenework. These notes can be used in staff meetings to review each member's case file. This can be done several times during the course of the program year. Out-of-group contact (e.g., phone calls, performances, individual therapy with interns, other meetings, or all of these) should be noted.

Confidentiality is maintained among the staff in a unique way: A group member must give permission for a staff member to discuss the group member's situation with any other adult or young person. Without that permission, group members are not discussed, even with parents or teachers. If a parent or teacher initiates contact with an AO staff person about a group member, suggest to that adult that you will contact the group member about this conversation to disclose the full contents of the meeting or phone call.

Although it is realized that many clinical settings could not follow this model, it is provided as a point of reference. It works well for us, and perhaps some aspects of it may work for your agency or setting as well.

WARM-UP ACTIVITIES

Warm-up activities help focus the group's attention. They can energize when the group is sluggish or contain when the group is too chaotic. Based on experience, channeling chaos is more effective than trying to stop it. A good warm-up either sets the tone for a productive group meeting or ends an intense meeting with some lightness and an ability to leave that energy behind in order to prepare for the next activity or class.

The following are a sampling of warm-up activities that can be used to help focus and energize a group. Many others can be found in the works cited in Part C, General References and Resources.

Circle Count-off

The leader says "one" and passes the word and energy to the person on either side. The second person says "two" and this continues around the circle. *Make eye contact with the person you are receiving from and passing to.* Continue counting in sequence around the circle until reaching the leader again.

Word Association

The leader passes any word (e.g., blue) to the person next in the circle, who, in turn, free associates with the word and passes this response (e.g., moon) to the next person. This flies around the circle for one revolution. *Trust that you will come up with something new as you pass it along, again making sure to maintain eye contact.*

Group Sentence

Beginning and ending with the same person, a sentence is created, one word at a time, as each person in the circle speaks in sequence. The group needs to be aware as the sentence is nearing its end and work together to achieve appropriate completion.

Group Story/Sentence Building

The goal is to build a coherent, if odd, story with WHO, WHAT, and WHERE.

1. On the first revolution, each person gets to add one word.
2. On the second revolution, each person gets to add two words.

3. On the third revolution, each person adds three words.
4. On the fourth revolution, each person adds two words.
5. The fifth revolution is back to one word per person.
6. The exercise should begin and end with the same person.

Zip Zap Zop

One person says "zip," claps his or her hands, and points energetically to someone across the circle. This second person says "zap," claps, and points to a third person who says "zop," claps, and points. The process continues, repeating the three words in sequence. This can be played as an elimination game.

Elephant, Donkey, 1776

The goal is to create circumstances for practicing complete attention and focus through a silly, active game. This also can be played as an elimination game.

1. Review the gestures for each of the following terms: elephant, create trunk with hands; donkey, create ears with hands; 1776, create flute with hands.
2. One person begins by saying "elephant" and making the gesture while looking at another person in the circle, hereby passing the turn to this person.
3. This person says "donkey," makes the gesture, and passes the turn by making eye contact with another person.
4. This person says "1776," does the gesture, and passes it to someone else.
5. This process continues.

Gibberish

The group is standing in a circle. The leader instructs the group simply to speak gibberish (nonsense sounds) out into space. One member speaks a sentence in gibberish and the person to his or her right translates it into English. The process continues along the circle so that everyone has a chance both to speak gibberish and to translate someone else's sentence.

Issue Tag

The leader asks for two volunteers to come to the center of the circle. The group decides on a relationship for this pair. They two are instructed to begin a scene together. Either of them could be tagged by any other group member at any moment during the improv and replaced, but the story or scene must continue to flow. Group members should be encouraged to try both roles during the course of this exercise. After a few minutes, the leader asks the couple and the group to bring the scene to a close. Processing can take place, and themes may be discussed.

Tell Me about the Time When . . .

The leader asks a member to "Tell me about the time when . . ." and concludes the request with a highly unlikely situation such as "you were asked to co-star in a film with _____ (a famous actor)," or "your eyebrow jumped off your face and ate your pet gorilla." The member answers spontaneously and without hesitation. He or she then turns to another member and makes a similar query.

Nondirected Chain Improv

Two players begin a scene about any topic. As the scene progresses, others may enter and leave at will, making any changes they desire (i.e., within the ground rules the group sets). Others also may freeze any scene, replace any or all current participants, and switch to a new topic or idea. The goal is to "go with the flow" and to work with whatever occurs in each improv. These scenes generally are quite short, but actors may be encouraged to let the scene unfold a bit before freezing or entering it to change it. Themes that arise during these improvs often may show where the group's needs and issues are, and leaders either may reintroduce these themes or ask the group to name these themes in order to choose the scenario categories for that group meeting.

Note: Warm-up activities are collected from many different sources, and many groups use similar warm-ups, often not knowing who the originators were. ACTING OUT would like to acknowledge the IRONDALE Project in New York City and REFLECTIONS Teen Theatre Company, Staci Block, Director, in Fair Lawn, NJ, for sharing many such activities.

ESTABLISHING YOUR OWN PROGRAM

Many earlier topics in this book discussed some of these elements, but in this section are outlined the primary procedures needed.

Establishing Realistic Goals

If you have read this entire workbook, you already have begun the process. A future step is to get colleagues and supervisors to review these materials, but first you must clarify your goals. Decide in what aspects of your current position you could implement some or all of these activities. What curricular, therapeutic, institutional, social, or all of these goals can you imagine being served by the implementation of this program?

Items Needed

One beauty of this program is that it is almost free. Besides this workbook (one for each leader is a must) and perhaps supplemental materials (which are available in most libraries), you will need a chalkboard or other large writing surface, tissues, a clock, and movable chairs and tables in a large enough space so that a circle can be formed. Then, playing space of approximately 10 feet by 16 feet will need to be created.

When you have familiarized yourself enough with these materials; gotten whatever other training, additional leadership, or support you require; and clarified your purposes and goals, you are ready to begin. At this point, all you need are courage and time.

Time Needed

Standard class periods of 45 to 55 minutes are ideal for this type of program in a school setting. Longer periods work as well, although a break may be needed. Periods of less than 45 minutes are not recommended. Each session may focus on one topic area and use several scenarios, although each scenario contains sufficient material for an entire session.

Where to Start

You, as leader, should decide whether or not to repeat specific scenarios, which ones to use, which sequence is most desirable, and how many sessions to spend on each topic area. When getting started, the recommendation is that you begin with those topic areas that are less emotionally charged for your particular group, and warm up to hotter issues as your group develops a way of working well together.

Processing Happenings and Keeping Others Informed

If you are working in a clinical setting, these activities can be used within a standard group session. Be sure to leave time for processing at the end of the action. Cognitive integration is an important part of expressive therapy and helps provide a cool down so that members can return to their daily routines in a less agitated state. If you are working in an inpatient setting, be sure to spend time sharing your plans with other staff, particularly those who will be with your group members immediately after group meetings.

Processing each scene, and sometimes certain warm-up activities, must be a regular part of each meeting. By participating themselves whenever appropriate, leaders create an atmosphere of communication and expectations of sharing.

Personal Growth Plans (PGPs)

If Personal Growth Plans (PGPs) (see earlier section of this chapter, Evaluating) are used, these may become a regular focus or touchstone for your meetings. Files in which you keep these and other materials for each member will be useful, if not required.

Administering and Evaluating

Administering and evaluating are connected, so review the Evaluating section of this chapter for ideas. Besides taking attendance, leaders often take notes during group meeting times to remind themselves of issues discussed, scenarios used, actors who participated, format or techniques employed, warm-ups used, and so forth. It is amazing what you forget once the meeting is over for that day; therefore, the recommendation is to take notes or record your sessions (with member permission, of course) for leaders to use to plan future meetings.

PART B
ISSUE-ORIENTED
SCENARIOS

Part B contains eight chapters, with each chapter devoted to a specific timely issue of concern to teenagers. Each issue has eight to ten scenarios with five basic considerations for each: Who, What, Where, What Would Happen If . . ., and Things to Think About.

At the beginning of each chapter is provided a list of scenarios for a given timely issue. These scenarios can be dramatized in any order. If needed, part or all of a scenario may be modified to be appropriate for those involved as participants—as actors, as observers, or both.

Resources—local, state, and national—need to be considered, and specific procedures for utilizing each need to be identified before starting the scenarios. These resources need to be discussed with participants. An illustrative list of resources is provided at the start of each chapter.

Chapter 5

DRUGS/ALCOHOL

List of Scenarios

- WOULD THIS HELP?: Using other people's medications.
- JUST TRY IT: Peer pressure to use drugs.
- LOOK WHAT I FOUND: Pre-teens and pot.
- NOT MY DRUGS: Kids, parents, and substance abuse.
- COCAINE COMRADES: Life history and drug use.
- ABOUT THAT $20: Borrowing money for drugs.
- BACK OFF: Confronting a friend about drug use.
- PARTY ON: Drug overdose at a party.
- MOM'S PROBLEM: An alcoholic parent.
- HI, DAD: Coming home drunk.
- ONE FOR THE ROAD: Drinking and driving.
- I DON'T KNOW WHAT HAPPENED: Results of drunk driving.

RESOURCES

Most communities have substance abuse prevention programs such as D.A.R.E., S.T.O.P.P., and police or school-related programs. In addition to those, check with your local or regional mental health agencies for residential treatment centers in your area and possible programs, brochures, or guest speakers that they could offer.

Also, these references may be useful: Alcoholics Anonymous and related support groups (Narcotics, Cocaine, and Marijuana often have separate sections); Al-Anon, for members of families of drug- or alcohol-related abuse problems of a parent or sibling or spouse.

Scenario: WOULD THIS HELP?

WHO

Jerry—is eight years old, has asthma, and is friends with Andy.

Andy—is 10 years old and has asthma, although it is a much milder case than Jerry's.

WHAT

Jerry and Andy are playing. It is a very hot, muggy day and they have been chasing each other for about 15 minutes. Suddenly Andy starts having trouble breathing. Jerry offers Andy a prescription inhaler.

WHERE

On the playground at school.

WHAT WOULD HAPPEN IF

Andy accepts the medication?
the medication makes Andy's breathing better?
a teacher sees Andy accept Jerry's medicine?
the medication makes Andy's breathing worse?
Andy doesn't accept the medication?
Andy's breathing gets worse?

THINGS TO THINK ABOUT

Why should Andy accept or not accept Jerry's medication?
What are some reasons that Jerry might offer his medication to Andy?
Is it dangerous to accept someone else's medication, even if you already have the same medicine prescribed to you?
If you have a headache and a friend offers you aspirin, should you accept? Why or why not?

Scenario: JUST TRY IT

WHO

Jesse and Pat—are students of whatever age is appropriate for those who have not used drugs before. Jesse is certain he or she is not interested in trying them and has a clear understanding of the reasons for this choice. Pat is curious about the possibility of experimenting with drugs. He or she is aware of the same information as Jesse but is uncertain that it really matters.

J.J. and P.J.—are students who are a little older and have used drugs in the past. They both believe that their current level of use is not a problem for them or anyone else. They enjoy the feelings they have while under the influence.

WHAT

The older students encounter the younger students. They offer Jesse and Pat the chance to try marijuana. They are quite insistent about it and use every argument they can think of. Jesse refuses but Pat is uncertain. After a while Jesse leaves, and Pat is left alone with J.J. and P.J. They increase the pressure. (This is a good point to introduce Pat's "angel and devil" inner voices to illustrate the choice process.)

WHERE

This scene takes place on an empty school playground after school.

WHAT WOULD HAPPEN IF

Pat decides not to try it?
Pat decides to try smoking pot, then goes home?
Pat has very few friends and longs for acceptance?
J.J. and P.J. are drug dealers?
Jesse returns with a police officer or teacher?
the drug in question is LSD, speed, cocaine, etc.?

THINGS TO THINK ABOUT

Why would the older students want the younger ones to try the drug?
What are the physical, emotional, and social effects of the drug in question?
Is the drug in question addictive or habit-forming?
What are the consequences of getting caught?
What are the consequences of being "in the presence of" people doing or possessing drugs if you are a minor?

Scenario: LOOK WHAT I FOUND

WHO

Jeri—is a pre-teen who admires his or her big brother and wants to be just like he is. Their parents both work and are out of the home often, leaving the older brother in charge.

Lee—is Jeri's best friend who lives next door. The two have spent a lot of time together since first grade.

WHAT

Jeri is home alone and has found some pot in the older brother's room. Lee stops by to play video games. Jeri shows Lee the pot and suggests they try some.

WHERE

In the basement rumpus room in Jeri's house.

WHAT WOULD HAPPEN IF

the two decide to put the pot back?
Jeri decides to confront brother about it?
either or both friends decide to try the pot?
one had tried it before?
they try the pot and one of them gets sick?
Jeri's brother comes home and finds them?
Jeri's parent(s) come home and find them with pot?
Lee's mother comes over to get Lee?
the drug in question was alcohol? cocaine? etc?

THINGS TO THINK ABOUT

What effects might pot have on younger children that are different from the effects on teens?
What choices might the friends consider in this situation?
Are older siblings responsible if younger siblings follow a negative example?
At what age are young people generally confronted with the opportunity to use pot and other drugs?

Scenario: NOT MY DRUGS

WHO

Parent—works all day during the week and loves Kid but often does not have much time to spend with his or her kid.

Kid—is any age, an "average kid" who gets along okay with Parent but wants to be left alone more.

WHAT

The parent finds a bag of marijuana in the kid's dresser. The kid is confronted with this when he or she gets home from school. The kid denies any knowledge of how the bag of pot got there.

WHERE

In the family kitchen on a school night.

WHAT WOULD HAPPEN IF

the drugs do, in fact, belong to the kid?
the kid admits or refuses to admit ownership?
the kid, in fact, knows nothing about the drugs?
the drugs belong to a friend and the kid knows or doesn't know that they were left there?
the drugs belong to a sibling or the other parent and the kid knows or doesn't know about it?
the other parent, sibling(s), or both are there too?
the confronting parent is a drug user or alcoholic?
the drug in question is cocaine, LSD, speed, etc.?

THINGS TO THINK ABOUT

What are the physical, emotional, and social effects of the drug in question?
What are some reasons a parent might use drugs?
Where can a substance abuser get help?
At what point does using drugs become a problem?
If drugs are found in a home by the police, who is legally responsible?
Can a parent have his or her child arrested for possession of drugs?
What are the laws concerning possession, use and sale of controlled substances in your state?

Scenario: COCAINE COMRADES

WHO

Jen—is a 17-year-old girl who grew up in a family that used drugs openly. She rolled joints for her parents when she was seven. She uses cocaine recreationally. Her use has been increasing recently.

Michelle—is a 16-year-old girl, fifth child and only girl in her family. Her mother left after she was born, and Michelle is expected to do all the work in the house. She will do anything to be accepted as part of a group.

Lauren—is a 17-year-old girl from a "perfect" family. Her parents are professionals and expect her to be perfect. She is looking for forms of escape.

Alex—is a 16-year-old girl who lives with her father and a brother who is 22. Alex's brother is a heavy user and sells drugs. He introduced her to cocaine when she was 10; she has developed a serious habit.

WHAT

The four girls just have taken a substance abuse survey at school and are discussing it. Jen is worried about her drug use. She shares her story and asks the other girls to share theirs. They speak in the order listed. Lauren then takes out some cocaine and offers it to the others. They ask where she got it as she was broke the day before. With coaxing, she reveals that she has had sex with Alex's brother for cocaine. The others react.

WHERE

At Lauren's house after school. Her parents are at work.

WHAT WOULD HAPPEN IF

one of the girls needed a fix during the scene?
some of the girls decide to quit using?
Alex reveals that her brother has been sexually abusing her as well?
all or some of the characters were boys?

THINGS TO THINK ABOUT

What are the effects of cocaine on the body? in the nervous system?
What are the different forms cocaine comes in?
What is cocaine withdrawal like?
Where could the girls go for help?

Scenario: ABOUT THAT $20

WHO

Terry—is a teen who has problems at home and at school, both social and academic, especially since entering high school.

Alex—has been best friends with Terry since the fourth grade. Alex is concerned that Terry seems to be avoiding contact with friends and is missing school and social events a lot.

WHAT

Terry borrowed money from Alex, who has come to be repaid as promised. Alex needs the money for tickets to a special concert. Terry makes excuses about not having the money. Alex notices that Terry's stereo system is gone and questions Terry about it, discovering that Terry has a cocaine habit.

WHERE

In Terry's room at home.

WHAT WOULD HAPPEN IF

Alex gets extremely angry with Terry about the money?
Alex is concerned and suggests Terry seek help?
Terry starts doing cocaine in front of Alex?
Terry offers Alex cocaine and he or she accepts? What if he or she declines?
one of the friends has a severe negative reaction to the cocaine?
Alex tells Terry's parent(s) about the problem?
Terry's parents use drugs also?
the drug in question is pot? LSD? Another drug?

THINGS TO THINK ABOUT

What are the physical, emotional, and social effects of cocaine?
Why might friends encourage each other to try cocaine?
Can people use cocaine and have control of their habit?
At what point does drug use become a problem?
What can happen if you just try cocaine once?
How expensive is cocaine and how might someone get the money needed to support a cocaine habit?

Scenario: BACK OFF

WHO

Jonathan—is 16 years old and moved to the neighborhood about a year ago. He quickly became friends with David who lives next door.

David—is also 16, has started to hang out with a new group of friends, and is getting high more and more.

WHAT

Jonathan has decided to confront David about his drug use. David is a very difficult person to confront and gets angry with Jonathan.

WHERE

In David's back yard after school.

WHAT WOULD HAPPEN IF

they get into a fight and David walks away?
David offers Jonathan some of his stash?
David admits that he is out of control and asks Jonathan to help him?
Jonathan threatens to tell David's parents, the police, or both about David's use?
David promises not use or be under the influence of drugs when he is with Jonathan?
both of the characters are females? One is a female and other one a male?
one of David's parents overhears their conversation?

THINGS TO THINK ABOUT

How might someone's behavior change when using drugs?
What is the difference between an addict and a casual user? How can you tell the difference?
What should Jonathan do if David does not listen to him?
What can David do if he decides to get help?

Scenario: PARTY ON

WHO

Four friends—Jo, Flo, Mo, and Bo, are seniors in high school. They have been part of the same crowd since eighth grade. For the past few years they have been drinking and smoking pot together on occasion. They are all average students in school and not one of them feels that his or her substance use is a problem.

WHAT

Jo's parents are away for the weekend, leaving Jo home alone. Jo has invited the friends over to party. They drink a few beers and smoke a few joints. Then Jo brings out some cocaine. None of the others has done cocaine before, and they all decide to try it. After a short while, Bo starts having a severe negative reaction to the drug.

WHERE

At Jo's house, in the living room.

WHAT WOULD HAPPEN IF

no one noticed the friend who was having an overdose?
the person who overdosed had to go to the hospital?
the parent(s) came home?
the person who overdosed was Jo?
the host of the party had a police record?

THINGS TO THINK ABOUT

At the time of doing drugs can people be rational enough to respond to an emergency?
If a guest at a party overdoses, who is liable?
Can you overdose the first time you do cocaine?
Can different people react differently to the same amount of a drug? Why?

Scenario: MOM'S PROBLEM

WHO

Mom—is in her mid- to late-30s and is an alcoholic. She neglects family responsibilities, which are her only work at this time, expecting her oldest child to take care of everything.

Dad—is in his late 30s and is a "professional." He works all day during the week, often coming home late. He takes little, if any, responsibility for household and family matters.

The kid—is in his or her mid-teens and is the oldest of two children. Because the kid takes care of the house and the sibling, he or she has to give up after-school activities and friends.

The sibling—is seven years old. He or she acts up in school.

WHAT

The kid is putting dinner on the table when Dad comes home. Mom is drunk and argumentative. The sibling tells the parents that they have to go see his or her teacher because of problems at school. The kid decides to confront the parents about the mother's alcohol problem.

WHERE

The family dining room.

WHAT WOULD HAPPEN IF

Dad refused to acknowledge Mom's problem?
Dad acknowledges Mom's problem but she won't?
the sibling starts acting up?
the family begins to come to terms with their problem?
the kid talks to a guidance counselor about what's going on at home?

THINGS TO THINK ABOUT

Why might the mother have started to drink?
What can the kid do to encourage a change?
Where could the family go for help?
What are some ways that alcohol and drug abuse impact families?
What can young people do if there is a problem such as this one at home and the parents will not do anything about it?

Scenario: HI, DAD

WHO

Dad—is a recently divorced man who is doing his best to be a single parent. He works two jobs and is seldom home.

Son—has just entered high school and is trying to fit in. He is upset by his parents' divorce but tends to hold in his feelings rather than look for support.

WHAT

Son comes home drunk, one hour past his curfew. Dad is just getting home from work.

WHERE

At home in the kitchen.

WHAT WOULD HAPPEN IF

instead of a father and son, it is a mother and daughter? A mother and son? A father and daughter?
this is the first time it happened?
this happens regularly?
the father is an alcoholic?
the mother, who is no longer around, is an alcoholic?
the parent is understanding? unreasonable?

THINGS TO THINK ABOUT

When does alcohol use become a problem?
What are the consequences if a minor is caught drinking?
What health factors are involved with drinking?
Who is more likely to become an alcoholic? Is it hereditary?

Scenario: ONE FOR THE ROAD

WHO

> Brother—is a senior in high school and likes to hang out and party with his friends. He is annoyed that he has to provide rides for his younger sister.

> Sister—is an eighth-grader who is involved in after-school sports.

WHAT

> The brother has been drinking with his friends and had one for the road before picking up his sister from a junior high basketball game. The sister smells the alcohol as she gets in the car and confronts her brother about it.

WHERE

> In the parked car outside of the gym.

WHAT WOULD HAPPEN IF

> the brother decides to drive home even though he has had too much to drink?
> the brother gets caught drinking and driving?
> the sister gets out of the car and calls her parents for a ride?
> driving home with her brother is the only ride she has because her parents are out for the evening?
> the sister is older and also has a driver's license?

THINGS TO THINK ABOUT

> Who is responsible for the decision to ride with an impaired driver?
> How many drinks is too many before it affects one's driving ability?
> What happens if someone is caught drinking and driving?
> What are some tactics for preventing an impaired driver from driving?

Scenario: I DON'T KNOW WHAT HAPPENED

WHO

Jo—is a junior in high school who likes to hang out and drink with friends. Jo recently has gotten a driver's license.

Jesse—is a junior in high school and is a friend of Jo's. Jesse does not have a license yet so is dependent on others for rides.

WHAT

Jesse and Jo stop for a bite after school and talk about a party the afternoon before, at which everyone was drinking heavily. Jo doesn't remember much, only driving home and dodging a person on a bike. The next thing he or she remembered was waking up for school, afraid that he or she may have hit the biker.

WHERE

At a local fast food restaurant.

WHAT WOULD HAPPEN IF

Jess has information that a biker was hit on the road to Jo's house yesterday evening.
the person Jo hit was injured? dead?
the biker was a close friend of Jesse's? Jo's?
no one knows it was Jo who hit the biker? (What would Jo do? What would Jesse do?)
Jo's car was identified by a witness, and the police come to the restaurant to question Jo?

THINGS TO THINK ABOUT

Who is liable for Jo's actions?
How much alcohol can a driver consume and still drive safely?
Is it possible not to remember something while you're drunk?
What are the consequences Jo will face if the biker is injured? dead?
At what point is a driver considered legally Driving While Intoxicated?
How is this determined by the police?
What other DWI laws are you aware of? (Driving Under the Influence [DUI] is also usable here.)

Chapter 6

HIV AND OTHER STDs

List of Scenarios

- WHAT CAN I DO?: Teen tells friend that he or she has an STD.
- NO, I CAN'T: Teen refuses to become sexually involved because of STD infection.
- WE HAVE TO TALK: Teen tells lover that he or she has an STD.
- UNCLE STEVE: Victim of childhood sexual abuse learns that perpetrator has AIDS.
- I'LL BE OK: Single parent goes into hospital with AIDS-Related-Complex (ARC).
- WHAT ABOUT THE BABY?: Pregnant girl learns that the father of her baby is HIV-Positive.
- HELP!: Teen tells parents that he or she is HIV-Positive.
- I NEED MY JOB: Food server tells boss he or she is HIV-Positive.
- WHO COULD IT BE?: Students discuss the rumor that someone in their school is HIV-Positive.
- NOT IN OUR SCHOOL: Parents react to HIV-Positive student in their children's school.

RESOURCES

Most communities have Planned Parenthood, Family Planning, local hospitals, or clinics that offer STD and HIV testing and education; colleges and universities are especially well-equipped with hand-outs and information that

47

you could tailor to your age group. In addition to those, check with your local or regional medical agencies for free treatment centers in your area and possible programs, brochures, or guest speakers that they could offer.

HIV/AIDS hotlines are available in most calling areas. Check with your 800 operator (1-800-555-1212). Also, these references may be useful: *Changing Bodies, Changing Lives* (1980 and updates), Bell et al., Boston, MA, Teen-book Project; and *The Playbook for Kids about Sex* (1980), Blank & Quackenbush, Burlingame, CA, YES press.

Scenario: WHAT CAN I DO?

WHO

Ray—is 17 years old. He has a girlfriend named Kathy and has been dating her for about eight months. She told him last night that he needed to get tested for chlamydia. He is extremely embarrassed because, for one thing, he doesn't even know what chlamydia is or where to go to get tested.

Robin—is also 17 years old. She has been best friends with Ray for years. She knows a little about STDs and how to take care of them.

WHAT

Ray and his girlfriend had sex for the first time last month, and he didn't know that she had an STD. In fact, they had never even talked about their sexual backgrounds. Now Ray has to be tested for something. He has no idea what it is or how dangerous it is. He confides in his friend, Robin.

WHERE

Walking home to Robin's house after school.

WHAT WOULD HAPPEN IF

Kathy had not told Ray that she was infected, but he heard it from someone else? from Robin?
Robin doesn't know how to help Ray?
Ray is too embarrassed to get tested?
Robin is too embarrassed to talk to Ray about it?

THINGS TO THINK ABOUT

What are the symptoms of chlamydia?
How is chlamydia cured or treated?
How is this disease transmitted?
Is it necessary to be tested to really know if you have it?
Should people talk to each other about their sexuality before they have sex with each other?
How could you protect yourself from transmitting or receiving chlamydia?
Is this a bacterial or viral infection? What is the difference?

Scenario: NO, I CAN'T

WHO

Carly—is 17 years old. She started a relationship with Jim about six months ago. She has been sexually active in the past but has not yet had intercourse with Jim.

Jim—is also 17 years old. He wants to have sex with Carly and is aware that she has had intercourse before.

WHAT

Carly can't have unprotected or unsafe sex with Jim because she is about to have an outbreak of herpes. Carly contracted herpes from an old boyfriend. She was not aware that he was infected at the time. She is afraid to tell Jim because she wants to continue their relationship.

WHERE

In Jim's room after school. His parents are not home.

WHAT WOULD HAPPEN IF

Carly tells Jim why she can't have certain types of sex with him?
Carly just tells Jim that she doesn't want to have sex but won't tell him why?
Jim tells Carly that if she doesn't tell him why he'll break up with her?
Carly tells Jim the truth and he gets angry and wants to end the relationship?
Carly tells Jim and he is understanding?

THINGS TO THINK ABOUT

How is herpes contracted?
What are its effects?
Is it safe for people with herpes to have all types of sex? Why or why not?
How is herpes treated?
Can it be cured?
How does an infected person know that he or she is about to have an outbreak? Is this true in all cases?

Scenario: WE HAVE TO TALK

WHO

Jordan—is 17 years old and in the 11th grade. Last week he went to a party and drank too much. He had sex with Becki who was also drunk. Jordan had never had sex with anyone before. He did not think too much about it, thinking Becki probably would not even talk to him again.

Becki—is also 17. She had to ask a friend what happened at the party because she could not remember. She was horrified when she realized what had happened.

WHAT

Becki asks Jordan to meet her after school. She has to tell him that she has gonorrhea. She contracted it from her ex-boyfriend who told her that he had not had sex with anyone else.

WHERE

In the back parking lot after school.

WHAT WOULD HAPPEN IF

Jordan is embarrassed to talk to Becki, and he tries to avoid the conversation?
Jordan has a steady girlfriend and they had sex before Becki could tell Jordan?
they had or had not used a condom when they had sex?
Becki had been HIV-positive instead of having gonorrhea?
the situation had been reversed and it was Jordan who initially was infected?

THINGS TO THINK ABOUT

What is gonorrhea and how does it affect women? men?
How is it treated?
Does wearing a condom protect you from contracting it?
Can the infection be transmitted before the infected person shows symptoms?
How long after contact do the symptoms occur?
How long do you have to wait before gonorrhea can be detected by a test?
Can gonorrhea be transmitted in any other ways than intercourse?

Scenario: UNCLE STEVE

WHO

The kid—is a teenager who had been abused sexually when he or she was 11 by Uncle Steve. He or she has been in therapy but still has a lot of unresolved issues. He or she has tried to put this past episode out of mind, but memories still resurface from time to time.

The parent—knew about the abuse but did not bring charges at the time. The family moved; Uncle Steve is now 2,000 miles away. The parent loves the kid, and feels that the abuse is over and should be forgotten. The other parent died several years ago.

WHAT

The parent finds out that Uncle Steve is in the hospital with AIDS-related complications. The parent tells the kid and suggests that the kid get tested.

WHERE

In the family living room.

WHAT WOULD HAPPEN IF

the kid is or has been sexually active?
Uncle Steve is dead parent's or living parent's sibling?
Uncle Steve was not a relative but a Vietnam war buddy of the kid's father?
the kid never told anyone about having been abused by Uncle Steve?
the kid tests positive or negative?

THINGS TO THINK ABOUT

What are the ways HIV can be transmitted?
What is the difference between HIV and AIDS?
How is an HIV test performed and what does it test for?

Scenario: I'LL BE OK

WHO

The father—was divorced seven years ago because his wife was unfaithful. He works two jobs to support his two children. He has been sick a lot in the past few months.

Jazz—is 15 years old. She was very angry with her parents for getting a divorce until she found out why. Now she works part-time so she can buy her own clothes and have her own spending money.

Larry—is 12 years old. He was not told why his father divorced his mother and still hopes that they will get back together. He has not seen his mother since the divorce.

WHAT

The father has just come home from the doctor's office where he was told that his HIV test was positive. The doctor has insisted that he go into the hospital for further testing and treatment. He has obviously been infected for some time. He has to tell the children he needs to be hospitalized but is uncertain what else to say.

WHERE

In the living room, after the children get home from school.

WHAT WOULD HAPPEN IF

the father does or does not tell them why he is going to the hospital?
the father does or does not tell them that he was infected by their mother?
he had not been infected by their mother but by a lover he had after the divorce?

THINGS TO THINK ABOUT

What is the difference between HIV-positive and AIDS?
What does the T-cell count have to do with the different stages of AIDS?
Do physical exertion and stress affect how sick a person with HIV or AIDS will get?
Is there any danger that the father may have infected his children by their all living in the same house?
What kinds of medical treatments may be recommended for people with HIV?

Scenario: WHAT ABOUT THE BABY?

WHO

The woman—is any age and is two months pregnant. She has not yet told
her lover that she is pregnant. She wants her baby very much.

The lover—is about the same age as the woman. He loves the woman but
has just found out that an old sexual partner is HIV-positive. He got tested
without telling the woman.

WHAT

The lover finds out that he is HIV-positive. He goes to tell the woman. When
he arrives she tells him that she is pregnant. He then tells her he is HIV-
positive.

WHERE

At the woman's home in the kitchen.

WHAT WOULD HAPPEN IF

the couple had always used a condom?
the lover is not the baby's father?
the lover had or had not told the woman of his previous sexual relationship.
the infected former lover was another man?

THINGS TO THINK ABOUT

If the woman tests negative at this point, could she still be, in fact, HIV-
positive? Why?

If the woman is, in fact, HIV-negative, could the baby still have be born
HIV-positive?

If the woman is HIV-positive, will the baby definitely be HIV-positive as
well?

Could the baby be tested before birth?

If the woman is HIV-positive and her baby is HIV-negative, is it safe for
her to breast-feed the baby?

Scenario: HELP!

WHO

Danny—is 18 years old. He or she has been sexually active for three years. Although Danny had access to information about HIV/AIDS, he or she did not pay much attention to it.

The mother—always has had a problem thinking about "her Danny" having sex. The topic makes her very uncomfortable.

The father—knows that Danny is sexually active and has told Danny that he does not want to hear about it. The father thinks that Danny is too young and should not be having sex.

WHAT

Danny found out that one of his or her partners has tested positive for HIV and went to get tested two weeks ago. Danny just received the positive results. Now Danny has to tell his or her parents and isn't quite sure how to do it.

WHERE

In the kitchen after Danny's parents return home from work.

WHAT WOULD HAPPEN IF

Danny doesn't tell his or her parents, but they had been told by a friend of theirs who works in the clinic where Danny was tested?

Danny's parents are or are not understanding and supportive?

Danny's parents refuse to pay for medical bills?

the mother is understanding but the father isn't? vice versa?

Danny contracted AIDS from a same-sex partner?

THINGS TO THINK ABOUT

If Danny doesn't have medical insurance, how could he or she get medical treatment?

If you were Danny, would you tell a friend before you told your parents?

Is it important for Danny's parents to know that he or she is HIV-positive?

Why is it important for teens to talk about AIDS/HIV with their parents?

What are the laws in your state regarding someone's disclosing another person's HIV status?

Scenario: I NEED MY JOB

WHO

Nicky—is 19 years old. He or she has worked at the Town Diner for two years. Nicky is a wonderful food server and does a great job. Nicky was diagnosed as HIV-positive two years ago, just after he or she started working at the diner.

The boss—doesn't know that Nicky has HIV. The boss appreciates what a good worker Nicky has been. Business has been slow lately and the restaurant is just making it.

WHAT

Nicky was bringing a food tray to a table when he or she accidentally tripped. He or she fell and cut his or her hand on a broken glass. The boss tried to help but was asked not to interfere. The boss is now confronting Nicky about the incident and Nicky decides to tell the truth.

WHERE

In the restaurant after lunch hour rush.

WHAT WOULD HAPPEN IF

the boss fires Nicky when he or she learns the truth?

Nicky doesn't tell the boss, but the boss had heard a rumor that Nicky is HIV-positive and confronts Nicky?

Nicky didn't fall, but one of the customers knows that Nicky is HIV-positive and makes a scene in the restaurant?

the boss wants to be supportive and is afraid of what customers might do if they learn about Nicky's HIV status?

THINGS TO THINK ABOUT

Is it dangerous for HIV-positive people to work in food service jobs? Why or why not?

How might the stress of a restaurant job affect the health of someone infected with HIV?

If Nicky is fired because of HIV status, does he or she have any legal recourse?

Scenario: WHO COULD IT BE?

WHO

JJ, Sam, Pat, and Fran—have been classmates ever since elementary school. Most of the time JJ and Pat disagree about political and moral issues. Generally they get along pretty well. JJ and Sam are very well informed about AIDS and other STDs, but Pat and Fran are not.

WHAT

Pat shares with the gang an overheard rumor that one of the students in their school is HIV-positive. They get into a discussion about whether or not they want someone with HIV in their school and speculate as to whom it could be.

WHERE

In the hallway before school.

WHAT WOULD HAPPEN IF

Pat and Fran are seriously afraid that they can catch HIV from this student? the HIV-positive student is one of these four? the HIV-positive student contracted the disease from a blood transfusion? fist fight? sexual conduct? drug use? the identity of the HIV-positive student is known by one of the people in the group and he or she tells or refuses to tell the others?

THINGS TO THINK ABOUT

What are high risk and low risk behaviors for contracting HIV? Is there any risk involved with casual contact between HIV-positive and HIV-negative individuals? Who is most at risk? What precautions are appropriate for an HIV-positive individual in a social environment such as school? How do we know that HIV cannot be transmitted through casual contact? Is it possible to be safe and compassionate when supporting HIV-positive individuals?

Scenario: NOT IN OUR SCHOOL

WHO

Marty—has two teens in the area schools. Marty is very involved in what goes on in the school.

Jack and Elisha—also have two teens in the high school. Although it is more difficult for them, they try to stay involved in the school. They have been neighbors with Marty's family for ten years.

Bobby and Corine—have a daughter in the high school. They just moved into the neighborhood about three months ago.

WHAT

Marty has invited the others to his or her house to talk about the issue of an HIV-positive student in the school before the PTO meeting tomorrow night. Jack and Elisha are afraid of the risk for their children. None of them is aware that the HIV-positive student is Bobby and Corine's daughter, Andrea.

WHERE

In Marty's home.

WHAT WOULD HAPPEN IF

Jack and Elisha decide to try to get the HIV-positive student kicked out of the school?

Marty invites a Community Health Educator to help them become more informed about HIV?

Corine tells the others it is Andrea?

Andrea comes to see her parents and hears their conversation?

the children in these families are in elementary school rather than high school?

THINGS TO THINK ABOUT

How can parents get educated about HIV/AIDS?

How can teens help educate their parents about HIV/AIDS?

Is it discriminatory to expel a student because he or she is HIV-positive?

Are noninfected students at any risk from being in school with an HIV-positive individual?

Is an HIV-positive individual at any risk from being in school with other youth?

Chapter 7

FAMILY PROBLEMS AND SITUATIONS

List of Scenarios

- ALL THE KIDS ARE WEARING . . . : Family financial pressures.
- THE TOYS: Conflict during play.
- BE HOME AT 10:00 Negotiating curfews
- THE REPORT CARD: Kids, parents, and grades.
- YOU'RE NOT MY FATHER: Kids and step-parents.
- I'M NOT A BABY: Negotiating more freedom.
- CAN I HAVE THE KEYS?: Kids and the family car.
- IT'S NOT MY FAULT: Sibling rivalry and blame.
- YOUR BROTHER WOULD NEVER . . . : Playing favorites.
- WE NEVER TOLD YOU, BUT . . . : Adoption.

RESOURCES

Most communities have affiliates of the State Department of Health and Human Services, which serve children and youth (DYF, DCYS, etc.). Social workers at these or local mental health agencies in your area may have information on programs, brochures, or guest speakers that they could offer.

There are also child abuse prevention and reporting hotlines available in most calling areas: check with your 800 operator (1-800-555-1212). Adoption agencies and organizations for adoptive parents, adoptees, and birth parents also offer information on these topics. Birthing centers and parenting support networks also offer classes and information about sibling relationships and similar topics.

Communication classes and references, sometimes called Parent Effectiveness Training (PET) or Talking with Your Teens, can be useful. If your community has a teen center, they may have resources that you could use. Also, family therapy references can offer additional exercises and insights.

Note: Reporting laws are quite strict and are designed to handle suspected child abuse or neglect. Please consult your local district or region's agencies for details.

Scenario: ALL THE KIDS ARE WEARING . . .

WHO

The mother—is in her mid-30s. She has been out of work for a long while. She just started working at a convenience store for minimum wage.

The father—is in his mid-30s. He quit school at 16. He is now working on his high school diploma. He also works for minimum wage.

The kid—is 12 and wants to be part of the "in" crowd. His or her wardrobe is limited and he or she has few of the things that the other kids in school have.

WHAT

The kid wants a pair of really expensive popular sneakers that the parents definitely cannot afford. The kid cannot understand why everybody else's parents can buy them trendy stuff.

WHERE

The food court of a local mall.

WHAT WOULD HAPPEN IF

the kid stole sneakers from a store and parents discovered it?
the kid stole money to buy the sneakers?
a parent stole the sneakers for the kid?
the kid saw a parent stealing something the family needed (food, etc.)?
a friend loaned the kid a pair of sneakers and the parents did not believe him or her?

THINGS TO THINK ABOUT

How might the parents feel about not being able to buy what the kid wants?
How else might the kid get the sneakers?
How much pressure is there in your school to wear certain kinds of clothes?

Scenario: THE TOYS

WHO

The girl—is about seven years old. She is an only child and lives with her mother and father. Both her parents work, so she often is left in the care of the next-door neighbor.

The boy—is also about seven. He is the youngest of four boys; his next oldest brother is five years older than he is. They live with their mom, a divorcee who works nights.

WHAT

The boy wants to go outside and play on the swing set. The girl wants to stay in and play video games. It is after school, and his mom has left for a short time to pick one of her sons up at soccer practice. Two other brothers are in their rooms doing homework.

WHERE

The boy's living room.

WHAT WOULD HAPPEN IF

the boy and girl got into a fight and one of the brothers intervenes?
mom comes home and discovers the fight?
one child always gives in to the other?
the boy wanted the girl to play football with him?
the girl wanted the boy to play dolls with her?
the boy and girl are brother and sister instead of neighbors?

THINGS TO THINK ABOUT

How can people resolve conflicts without fighting?
What are some other things the children might do in this situation?
Could they do something to satisfy both their wishes?
Do boys and girls have a more difficult time in situations like this than would two boys or two girls?

Scenario: BE HOME AT 10:00

WHO

Erin—is 13 years old. He or she is in the seventh grade and has been asking his or her parents for a later curfew. Erin is the oldest child in the family. Lately she has acquired a new group of friends.

The mother—is in her mid-30s. Mom is not sure she likes Erin's new friends. She is very unsure of how to guide Erin into appropriate choices without smothering Erin. They have had a good relationship in the past.

The father—is in his mid-30s. He also has mixed feelings about Erin's new friends, mostly because they push Erin to take risks. He knows that Erin has tried smoking cigarettes.

WHAT

Erin wants to go out with his or her friends to see a movie. Usually Erin would go to the early movie and be home by 10:00 p.m. Tonight Erin wants to go to the later show, which means that he or she would not get home until 11:00 or 11:30.

WHERE

The kitchen, just before Erin's friend, Jory, is picking Erin up.

WHAT WOULD HAPPEN IF

Erin's parents refuse to extend the curfew past 10:00?
Erin's parents consent to a later curfew but just for tonight?
Erin's parents disagree on whether or not to give the later curfew?
Erin's father brings up his concerns about Erin's smoking?
Jory comes in while the discussion is in progress.

THINGS TO THINK ABOUT

What are some ways that Erin could show his or her parents that he or she is trustworthy?
What time is an appropriate curfew for someone between 13 and 15 years old?
Is it normal to change crowds when you hit junior high?
How should parents and kids negotiate new boundaries?

Scenario: THE REPORT CARD

WHO

Robin—is 14 years old. Robin usually has A-B grades but had problems in chemistry and got a C −.

The mother—is in her late-30s and is a single parent. She is very strict about earning good grades. She has grounded Robin for low grades before.

WHAT

Robin wants to go to the dance at school this weekend. Robin is afraid that because of this chemistry grade, he or she will be grounded by Mother.

WHERE

In the living room after dinner.

WHAT WOULD HAPPEN IF

Robin doesn't show his or her mother the report card until after Mom gives permission to go to the dance?

Robin changes the grade on the report card and Mom does or does not notice?

Robin's mother grounds him or her for two weeks?

Robin's mother decides to let Robin choose the punishment for the low grade?

TO THINK ABOUT

What are the consequences of changing grades on report cards?

Would Robin be in more trouble if he or she waited until after the dance to give the report card to his or her mother?

What punishment should Robin choose for the low grade if his or her mother decides to give Robin a choice?

Is it fair for a parent to punish a child for a low passing grade?

What alternatives, other than punishment, might Robin explore to deal with the low grade in chemistry?

Scenario: YOU'RE NOT MY FATHER

WHO

Raymond—is 12 years old. His mother and father divorced two years ago, and then they each remarried. Raymond lives with his mother and stepfather; he does not get along with his stepfather.

Carl—married Raymond's mother six months ago. He is trying to get along with Raymond; however, Carl is a very strong-willed individual. He had no experience with children prior to this marriage.

Carol—is Raymond's mother. She had no idea that Raymond would have so many problems with Carl. She loves Raymond very much but wants a life with Carl as well.

WHAT

It is Saturday morning. Raymond wants to hang out with his friends today, but his mother and Carl planned a day out for the family. Mom is just about to give in to Raymond when Carl puts his foot down and says Raymond is going with them, period.

WHERE

In the kitchen just before it is time to go.

WHAT WOULD HAPPEN IF

Raymond decides to leave regardless of what his mother and Carl say.
Raymond tries to play his mother against Carl to get his way?
Carol decides that if Raymond doesn't start cooperating, then he can go inside now and pack to go live with his father?
the family finally talks about how they feel in this post-divorce, new-marriage situation?

THINGS TO THINK ABOUT

Why might Carl and Raymond have such a hard time getting along?
What might Carol do to make things easier for everyone?
What could Raymond and Carl do to try to get along?
How could Carl begin to gain Raymond's trust?

Scenario: I'M NOT A BABY

WHO

Lacie—16 years old. She has always been a level-headed person. She lives with the same rules and curfews she had when she was 14 and feels it is time for a change.

The father—is in his mid-30s. His wife died two years ago. He does his best as a single parent but feels uncertain about how to raise a daughter right.

WHAT

Lacie wants to go to a Halloween party at a friends house, but the party doesn't end until 11:30. Her current curfew is 10:00. Her boyfriend has offered her a ride home but she is not allowed to ride with teen drivers.

WHERE

In the kitchen.

WHAT WOULD HAPPEN IF

Lacie's father says she can't go?
Lacie's Father says she can go but has to be in by 11:00, and he will drive her?
Lacie's father is willing to renegotiate the rules?
Lacie has been late often with her current curfew?

THINGS TO THINK ABOUT

Is Lacie's father being overprotective? Why? Why not?
How can Lacie show her father that she is responsible enough for new rules?
What is a reasonable way for parents and teens to make decisions that allow the teens to develop a sense of responsibility?

Scenario: CAN I HAVE THE KEYS?

WHO

Dana—is 16 years old. Dana just got a driver's license and borrows the car as often as possible. He or she has a good relationship with his or her mother but is feeling very independent.

The mother—is a single parent. She works full-time during the week and squeezes a lot of errands in on Saturdays. She tries to cooperate with Dana on use of the car when possible.

WHAT

It is Saturday. Dana borrowed the car this morning and was asked to be back before 11:00 a.m. Mother did not tell Dana why she needed the car. Dana does not get back until 2:00 p.m., and the tank is on empty.

WHERE

In the garage after Dana returns home.

WHAT WOULD HAPPEN IF

Dana's mother grounds him or her from using the car for two weeks?
this isn't the first time that Dana has not been back on time?
the reason Dana is late is because he or she had a car accident?
Dana is only a half hour late?

THINGS TO THINK ABOUT

Is Dana taking advantage of the use of the car?
How can Dana and his or her mother come to a better agreement of when, where, and how Dana uses the car?
Should Dana be required to fill the gas tank when he or she is finished using the car?
What responsibilities should a teen be willing to assume when given access to the family car?

Scenario: IT'S NOT MY FAULT

WHO

Jerry—is eight years old. He is very close to his sister, even though they often fight.

Janis—is two years older than Jerry and loves him but feels that he always gets more attention because he is a boy.

The father—goes to work early so he can be home when Janis and Jerry get home from school. He tries to treat his children fairly but does not always succeed.

WHAT

While their father was making dinner, Janis went in to talk to him. He told her that they would talk after dinner. Disappointed, she returned to living room. Later, Jerry went to ask their father something and was not asked to leave. Janis felt jealous and angry. When Jerry returned to the living room, Janis "accidentally" tripped him. Jerry hit Janis back. During the struggle, they knocked over a lamp. The scene begins as father comes in the room to see what happened.

WHERE

In the living room before dinner.

WHAT WOULD HAPPEN IF

Jerry blames Janis for tripping him and Janis says that it was an accident and Jerry hit her for no reason?
Janis or Jerry takes the blame for the other?
the father punishes Janis and not Jerry or vice versa?
both of them are punished?
Janis admits that she is jealous, and the three of them talk about it?
the parent is a mother instead of a father?

THINGS TO THINK ABOUT

How could Janis have dealt with the situation better?
Have you ever felt jealous of a brother or sister? Why?
Might parents sometimes treat an older sibling differently from a younger one? How? Why?

Scenario: YOUR BROTHER WOULD NEVER . . .

WHO

Georgie—is in the fifth grade. Georgie is somewhat rambunctious and sassy. Unlike Chris, Georgie is not an athlete. He or she does not have much in common with their father and often feels left out.

Chris—is in the seventh grade. Chris plays on the baseball and soccer team and is interested in many of the same things as their father.

Cory—is the father. He is a single parent and has a hard time relating to Georgie. He doesn't mean to treat Chris differently, but he and Chris just get along better with one another.

WHAT

Cory has been attempting for a while to get Georgie to join a sports team at school. Finally, Georgie decided to join the soccer team. After three weeks, Georgie is having a hard time on the team and decides to quit. When Georgie tells Dad that he or she doesn't want to be on the team, Cory says that Georgie never can follow through on anything and should take a lesson from Chris about finishing things that he or she has started.

WHERE

In the kitchen when Georgie gets home from practice.

WHAT WOULD HAPPEN IF

Georgie tells his or her father that he or she only joined the team to please him?
Georgie tells Cory that he or she knows that he or she is a disappointment but he or she is not Chris?
Chris comes in and sticks up for Georgie?
after a little while, Cory starts to see things from Georgie's point of view?
Georgie and Chris are both girls? both boys? a boy and a girl?

THINGS TO THINK ABOUT

What might the father do to get to know his youngest child better?
How can a parent offer love and support fairly to children who are very different from one another?

Scenario: WE NEVER TOLD YOU, BUT . . .

WHO

Mother and Father—were not able to have children of their own. They adopted Jamie as an infant. They have been waiting for the right time to tell Jamie about the adoption.

Jamie—is 12 years old. Jamie gets along reasonably well with his or her parents. Jamie has a project due for school on "The History of My Family."

WHAT

Jamie tells his or her parents about the school project and asks them to fill out a questionnaire about their family. They decide that it is time to tell Jamie the truth.

WHERE

In the family room after dinner.

WHAT WOULD HAPPEN IF

Jamie is angry that this information was not shared sooner?
Jamie accepts the information and wants to meet his or her biological parents?
instead of the school project, Jamie had overheard relatives discussing the situation and confronts his or her parents about it?
the information were disclosed during an argument between Jamie and his or her parents?

THINGS TO THINK ABOUT

Should parents tell adopted children that they are adopted?
At what age is it appropriate for parents to discuss this information with their children?
Why might or might not adopted children want to meet their biological parents?
Who are the "real parents," those who raised Jamie or the biological parents?

Chapter 8

SCHOOL PROBLEMS AND SITUATIONS

List of Scenarios

- THE BULLY: Picking fights and unjust punishment.
- THE THIEF: Getting caught stealing from a locker.
- THE DOG ATE IT: Problems with homework.
- I'LL BE KICKED OFF THE TEAM: A failing grade puts an athlete in jeopardy.
- KATE & DUPLIKATE: Cheating on a test.
- YOU'RE WEIRD: Picking on kids at school.
- THE RIGHT CROWD: Social exclusion and cliques.
- THAT'S UNFAIR: A teacher shows favoritism.
- I'LL MISS YOU: One friend is going away to college; the other is not.
- THE S.A.T.: Pressure to get into college.

RESOURCES

Most communities have affiliates of the State Department of Health and Human Services which serve children and youth (DYF, DCYS, etc.). Social workers at these or local mental health agencies in your area may have information on programs, brochures, or guest speakers that they could offer. If your community has a teen center, they may have resources that you could use. Guidance counselors often have curricula that may have exercises to augment these scenarios.

Police departments often have officers who speak to children or teens about the laws that affect them, about community service programs, and about peer pressure. Many schools also offer mediation programs, peer counseling programs, or both that you can recommend to members of your group.

The National Association of Mediation Education (based in western Massachusetts, but with local and regional affiliates in many states) and the Re-Evaluation Counseling International Network (based in Seattle, WA, but with branches in every state and most Westernized countries) offer classes, school and community programs, and literature on these topics. Also, family therapy references can offer additional exercises and insights.

Scenario: THE BULLY

WHO

John—is a bully at school who picks on other kids. He is careful to keep a low profile when teachers are around and does not usually act out in class.

Eric—has gotten into some trouble in school before. He is often late for classes and doesn't always turn his homework in on time. He is popular with other students and treats them with respect.

Teacher—is caring and committed to the students. He or she is very busy. As the end of the marking period is near, he or she has a lot of paper work to catch up on.

WHAT

John is picking a fight with Eric. Eric stands up for himself verbally. John hits Eric. In return, Eric hits John. The teacher comes in just in time to see Eric hit John. (Acting note: This scene is *not* about a fight; it is about the consequences. Actors should be coached accordingly.)

WHERE

In the hall after lunch on the way back to class.

WHAT WOULD HAPPEN IF

the teacher came in time to see the entire interaction?
the teacher did not walk by at all?
it is the principal who sees the interaction?
Eric does not react by hitting John?
the interaction does not lead to any physical confrontation?
the scene takes place with two girls?

THINGS TO THINK ABOUT

What other ways can someone handle a bully?
Why do some kids behave as John does?
What kind of student is most likely to be picked on by someone like John?

Scenario: THE THIEF

WHO

Jacob—is a 14-year-old who gets into trouble a lot in school.

Principal—is new on the job, is trying hard to be fair, and is not always certain how to respond.

WHAT

Jacob saw a girl standing two lockers down from his put a CD into her locker, but she did not close and lock her locker securely. During the next period, Jacob asks for a pass to the bathroom. Before returning to class, he takes the CD from the girl's locker. The principal is in the hall, sees Jacob, and confronts him. Jacob gives an explanation that is not honest.

WHERE

In the hall during classes.

WHAT WOULD HAPPEN IF

the principal believes Jacob?
the principal doesn't believe him and brings him to the office? calls in his parents?
the principal brings the girl into the office and asks Jacob to return the CD and apologize?
Jacob had seen the CD fall out of the locker and then had gone to take it.

THINGS TO THINK ABOUT

What is an appropriate consequence for stealing another person's property in school?
Why might someone steal?
If we leave our things around and someone takes them, is that person stealing?

Scenario: THE DOG ATE IT

WHO

Jackie—is 12 years old. He or she is in the seventh grade, is a very bright student, but is losing interest in school.

Social studies teacher—knows that Jackie has much more ability than he or she has been showing lately.

WHAT

For the fourth day in a row, Jackie has not turned in homework. Jackie's teacher is very concerned and asks Jackie to remain after class.

WHERE

The teacher's classroom after class.

WHAT WOULD HAPPEN IF

Jackie does or does not respond to the teacher's concern?
the reason Jackie is falling behind is due to some problem at home?
the teacher calls in Jackie's parents?
Jackie's grades have dropped in all his or her classes, not just social studies.
Jackie were not a good student but usually an all-around poor student?

THINGS TO THINK ABOUT

Why do some students lose interest in school?
What can the teacher do to get through to a student?
What do students lose by not participating in class assignments?
What are some ways that teachers and students can communicate better about schoolwork?
What is a reasonable amount of homework for a teacher to give?

Scenario: I'LL BE KICKED OFF THE TEAM

WHO

Carney—is in the tenth grade, on the soccer team, is a star player, and is very proud of his or her ability.

History teacher—is known to be very difficult and gives a lot of homework.

Parent—is very proud of Carney's ability and doesn't believe that Carney should be kicked off the soccer team for one bad quarter.

WHAT

The school rules say that an athlete must maintain a "C" average to remain on any athletic team. It is just before second quarter report cards. Carney finds that he or she is two points below a "C" because of his or her history grade. What will Carney do about soccer? One of Carney's parents goes with Carney for a conference with the teacher.

WHERE

In the teacher's classroom after school.

WHAT WOULD HAPPEN IF

the teacher absolutely refuses to try to work with Carney about his or her grade?

Carney asks the teacher for an extra-credit assignment to bring his grade up so his or her average will be a C.

the teacher agrees or does not agree to the extra credit.

the parent decides that if the teacher does not give Carney a passing grade, then he or she will pull Carney out of that class.

the teacher, after listening to Carney and the parent, decides to give Carney the passing grade.

THINGS TO THINK ABOUT

If Carney missed homework assignments and didn't take the class seriously, does he or she deserve a break?

Would taking Carney out of that class help or hurt Carney? What about Carney's other "D's" that pulled the average down for the quarter?

Should the teacher just give Carney the grade because he or she is an athlete?

Why are there school rules governing an athlete's right to play school sports on the basis of grades?

Scenario: KATE & DUPLIKATE

WHO

Kate—is in the eighth grade. She is a very bright student in math; at times, she even tutors other people in her class. Her favorite "student" is Milly, who sits next to her. Milly is very popular and Kate likes to help her, because it makes Kate feel important.

Milly—is at times a bit stuck-up, but usually she is nice. She is the joker of the class. For some reason, she doesn't like math and, therefore, doesn't try very hard.

Teacher—knows that Kate helps Milly with her work and is concerned about Milly taking advantage of Kate.

WHAT

There is going to be a test in math. Milly asks Kate to give her the answers to the questions on the test. Kate feels guilty about letting Milly cheat off her but doesn't want to seem square or uncool.

WHERE

On the way to math class, just before the test.

WHAT WOULD HAPPEN IF

Kate agrees or does not agree?
the teacher catches Kate giving the answers to Milly?
the teacher catches Milly taking answers from Kate's test?
Kate and Milly don't get caught?
Kate decides at the last minute not to let Milly cheat from her?
the teacher guesses what is going on and calls them to his or her desk during the test?

THINGS TO THINK ABOUT

What are your school's rules about cheating?
Was it fair of Milly to ask Kate to help her cheat?
Would it be better for Kate to tell Milly she wouldn't help her?
If Kate didn't help Milly, would she still be her friend?
How do you feel about cheating?

Scenario: YOU'RE WEIRD

WHO

Jay—is in the fifth grade and is not very popular, does not have the "best" clothes all the time, and is very quiet. Jay's father left when he or she was five, and Mom has a hard time providing. Jay has very low self-esteem and believes that everything others say when they are picking on him or her is true.

Andie—is also in the fifth grade. Andie is very popular and a ringleader in the class. Andie is not always a nice person, and often picks on classmates or puts them down for not being cool.

Ant—is also a very popular student, is most always kind, and is a favorite among students and teachers, hence the nickname (can be short for Antonia or Anthony).

WHAT

Andie is outside during recess and sees Jay sitting alone. Andie goes over and says something very mean about the way Jay is dressed. Ant hears the things that Andie is saying and comes to offer Jay support.

WHAT WOULD HAPPEN IF

because Ant helped Jay, Andie begins picking on Ant too?
a teacher sees what is happening and comes to help Jay?
other students join in?
Jay takes a stand and tells Andie how it feels to be picked on?

THINGS TO THINK ABOUT

How does being teased affect the way we feel about ourselves?
Is there some way to get students like Andie to stop picking on others?
Why do some students pick on others?

Scenario: THE RIGHT CROWD

WHO

Mel—is a little weird. Mel is very insecure; at times Mel likes himself or herself very much, and sometimes feels as if he or she really doesn't belong anywhere.

J.J.—fairly popular with many different people, is friends with Mel, but is easily swayed by the crowd.

WHAT

J.J. was with the popular crowd yesterday and joined them in ignoring and making nasty comments about Mel. Mel heard some of the things that J.J. was saying. This morning, Mel avoided J.J. and is sitting by himself or herself at lunch. J.J. doesn't have any idea why Mel is doing this.

WHERE

The school cafeteria.

WHAT WOULD HAPPEN IF

Mel tells J.J. what he or she heard and says that he or she doesn't want to spend time with J.J. anymore?
J.J. figures out what is wrong and apologizes?
Mel starts yelling at J.J.?
J.J. decides that it isn't worth trying to get Mel to talk to him or her, and says so?
Mel decides to tell J.J. that he or she is very hurt by the things that J.J. said?

THINGS TO THINK ABOUT

Is J.J. being a good friend? Why or why not?
What do you do when two friends you have don't like each other?
How could J.J. reconcile the differences between the two groups of people he or she hangs out with?
Could the things that J.J. said about Mel affect the way Mel feels about himself or herself?
How might it feel to be excluded from social circles?

Scenario: THAT'S UNFAIR

WHO

Mrs. Michelson—is a third-grade teacher. She knows that she needs to treat her students fairly, but this year one particular little girl is so "good" that Mrs. Michelson absolutely adores her. Her name is Judy.

Judy—is very popular. She always gets her work done and is naturally inquisitive. She speaks only when appropriate and is a very "beautiful" (traditional) little girl.

WHAT

Often Mrs. Michelson offers extra activities to her students. Today she needed someone to go pick up an envelope from the office, and two people raised their hands—Judy and Myn. As usual, Mrs. Michelson chose Judy. Myn yelled out that Mrs. Michelson wasn't being fair since she always picked Judy more than anyone else in the class. Very calmly, Mrs. Michelson asked Myn to return to his or her work. At recess, Judy goes to talk to the teacher about the fact that all the students are beginning to call her the "teacher's pet."

WHERE

In the classroom during morning recess.

WHAT WOULD HAPPEN IF

Judy explains to Mrs. Michelson that she doesn't like being chosen all the time, because then she is picked on?
Mrs. Michelson makes a deal with Judy that she won't call on her as much?
Myn is very angry and stays to talk to Mrs. Michelson also?
Myn were as good and cooperative as Judy?
Myn was the class troublemaker?

THINGS TO THINK ABOUT

Is Mrs. Michelson really showing favoritism or just rewarding good behavior?
Have you ever had a teacher who played favorites? (No names, please.)
How might students feel if a teacher plays favorites?

Scenario: I'LL MISS YOU

WHO

Loren—is going some distance away for college. This move is going to be very difficult. Loren's best friend, Lee, wanted to go to the same school but was not accepted; she will be going to a local school instead.

Lee—is very disappointed and upset that Loren is leaving. They have been friends since the third grade.

WHAT

The two are talking about leaving each other. They feel strange because they have never really done anything big without each other. Lee is depressed about having to stay closer to home for college, without Loren.

WHERE

In Loren's room on the night before he or she is going to leave.

WHAT WOULD HAPPEN IF

Lee had been accepted but could not afford tuition?
Loren has been thinking about not going if Lee isn't able to go also?
Lee asks Loren not to go?
Lee decides to put off school for a year and move in with Loren?
Loren suggests that Lee spend his or her first year at college at home then try to transfer?
Lee is a little bitter and jealous because things always seem to work out better for Loren?
Loren is happy, excited, and a little scared about going so far away and not knowing anyone, but Lee is only concerned about his or her own feelings of being left behind, so they fight?

THINGS TO THINK ABOUT

Is it good to be separated from friends for a while?
Is it okay for Lee to be a little jealous of Loren?
Should Loren change his or her mind about going because Lee can't go?
Should Lee put off going to school for a year so the two of them can be together?
What if this scene were taking place when Loren came home from college during winter break? What would they talk about? Would they still be good friends?

Scenario: THE S.A.T.

WHO

Mr. Fiscarro—is a guidance counselor. He has been helping Cory get ready for college for the past six months. He is having trouble getting Cory to take the S.A.T. seriously.

Cory—is in the 12th grade. He or she is not looking forward to the S.A.T. at all. The thought of taking the test makes Cory extremely nervous. Cory is not even sure that he or she wants to go to college.

WHAT

Mr. Fiscarro has a booklet that Cory can practice with, but Cory is being very difficult about practicing. Mr. Fiscarro is rather annoyed with Cory and is losing patience because he is not used to this almost non-caring attitude from Cory.

WHERE

In the guidance office at school.

WHAT WOULD HAPPEN IF

Cory becomes angry and storms out of the room?
Mr. Fiscarro gets annoyed and tells Cory that if he or she doesn't stop goofing off, then he will not help?
Cory tells Mr. Fiscarro that he or she is very nervous about the test?
Cory reveals that he or she is uncertain about going to college but is being pressured by family and friends?

THINGS TO THINK ABOUT

Why do students have to take the S.A.T.?
Should students go to college even if they are uncertain they want to go?
From where do the pressures to attend college come?
What options are available for those who do not attend college or who wish to postpone enrollment?
What about finding colleges that do not require the S.A.T. for admission (for people who hate those types of tests or who do not do well on them)?

Chapter 9

COMMUNITY PROBLEMS AND SITUATIONS

List of Scenarios

- A SWEATER FOR AMY: Boyfriend needs birthday gift for girlfriend.
- WALK ON THE WILD SIDE: Group acceptance.
- THE RIVALS: Students from rival schools at a community dance.
- THE NEW FRIEND: Racism/bigotry in the home.
- WE DON'T WANT THEM: Racism/bigotry at school.
- THE SCHOOL BOARD MEETING: Voicing beliefs in a public forum.
- BUT HE'S GOT NO PLACE TO GO!: Homelessness.
- THE INTERVIEW: Applying for a job.
- THE SOUP KITCHEN: Volunteering in the community.
- THE HUMANE SOCIETY: The plight of unwanted animals.

RESOURCES

Most communities have affiliates of the State Department of Health and Human Services that serve children and youth (DYF, DCYS, etc.). Social workers at these or local mental health agencies in your area may have information on programs, brochures, or guest speakers that they could offer. If your community has a teen center, they may have resources that you could use. Guidance counselors often have curricula that may have exercises to augment these scenarios.

Police departments often have officers who speak to children or teens about the laws that affect them, about community service programs, and about peer pressure. Many schools also offer mediation programs, peer counseling programs, or both that you can recommend to members of your group.

The National Association of Mediation Education (based in western Massachusetts, but with local and regional affiliates in many states) and the Re-Evaluation Counseling International Network (based in Seattle, WA, but with branches in every state and most Westernized countries) offer classes, school and community programs, and literature on these topics. Also, family therapy references can offer additional exercises and insights.

Scenario: A SWEATER FOR AMY

WHO

>Jason—is a teen with no job. He has liked Amy for some time but only recently got up the nerve to ask her out. Their relationship is off to a good start. Amy's birthday is coming up in a week.

>Mark—is a teen and is Jason's friend. Jason has been an important support person for Mark and has stood by him through some difficult family problems.

WHAT

>Jason wants to get Amy a sweater for her birthday. He knows she would like it, but he doesn't have enough money. He asks Mark to distract the sales person while he steals the sweater.

WHERE

>Outside a store in a mall, a week before Amy's birthday.

WHAT WOULD HAPPEN IF

>Mark refused and left the mall?
>Jason and Mark are caught and their parents have to get them from the police station?
>Jason is successful but feels guilty and wants to return the sweater?
>Amy does not like the sweater and tries to exchange it?
>Jason is successful and gives the sweater to Amy?
>she loves it, but it is the wrong size? she asks where he got it so she can exchange it?

THINGS TO THINK ABOUT

>What will happen to Jason if he is caught?
>Will Mark be in trouble if Jason gets caught?
>How else could Jason get the sweater? (He has a week until the birthday.)
>What other options might Jason have for Amy's birthday gift?

Scenario: WALK ON THE WILD SIDE

WHO

> Group of teenagers—want to be accepted by each other. (There is little available for teens in their community. None of them is into sports.)
> Ian—is a kid who wants to be part of the group but feels guilty for going along with the group's ideas of fun.

WHAT

> In order to be part of the group, the members dare each other to soap windows on Main Street late at night.

WHERE

> In an alley by Main Street.

WHAT WOULD HAPPEN IF

> Ian agrees to participate? refuses to participate?
> Ian is new in town and has no friends?
> the others get caught? don't get caught?
> Ian gets caught soaping windows?
> Ian reports the group members for soaping windows?
> the group decides to break windows also?
> one of the group members gets hurt?

THINGS TO THINK ABOUT

> What are the consequences for soaping windows? breaking windows?
> How likely is it that the first activity might lead to the second?
> What else could the group do to have fun?
> If some members are caught, should they tell who the others are?

Scenario: THE RIVALS

WHO

Cory and Jamie—go to Low Meadow High School. They are both on sports teams and are very spirited and loyal to their school. Both of them are keyed up for the big football game against High Meadow next week.

Adrian and Sam—go to High Meadow High School. They also are very spirited and loyal to their school. Adrian is the quarterback for the High Meadow football team.

WHAT

The biggest game of the year is the High Meadow versus Low Meadow football game. It seems as though whenever this game comes around, the already-heated emotions of students from both schools reach a boiling point. The school administrators from both schools decided to hold a community dance so that students from both schools would mix together and hopefully alleviate some of the hostility. The idea seemed to work until Jamie and Adrian started a discussion on which football team was going to win the game.

WHERE

At the town hall in Bounty (the town between those in which the two schools are located).

WHAT WOULD HAPPEN IF

Adrian insulted the Low Meadow football team? Jamie insulted the High Meadow team?
one of the four actually complimented the efforts of an opposing team member?
an adult heard the conversation and noticed how heated it was becoming?
another student heard it and stepped in?
this group was comprised of all males? all females? a mix of males and females?

THINGS TO THINK ABOUT

Why is there so much rivalry between schools, communities, countries?
Is this type of behavior encouraged in our society? In what ways? Who benefits? Who is harmed?

Scenario: THE NEW FRIEND

WHO

Nick—is in junior high. He or she gets along well with a wide range of students and enjoys making new friends.

Hio-lee—is also in junior high. His or her parents are teachers and have been looking for a school where they both could work. When they found and accepted jobs at Nick's school, Lee (as Hio-lee likes to be called) not only had to change schools but had to move over 100 miles from all his or her friends.

Gabriel—is Nick's father and is in his mid-50s. Although Gabriel does not let Nick see it, Gabriel feels that no "Eastern foreigners" should be allowed into the country, especially after America's experiences with Vietnam.

WHAT

It is Friday night. Nick has invited some friends over for a party for Lee so that he or she has the opportunity to meet more people. Because Lee is an "American" name, Nick's father did not realize that Lee is "Eastern." Once Gabriel meets Lee, he asks Nick to see him in the kitchen.

WHERE

In the kitchen during the party.

WHAT WOULD HAPPEN IF

Gabriel tells Nick that he or she has to tell everyone to go home?
Gabriel tells Nick that, after tonight, he or she is not allowed to have Lee over anymore?
Lee accidentally overhears their conversation?
Lee were from some other ethnic background? another religion? a lower social class? a minority sexual orientation?

THINGS TO THINK ABOUT

Where do racism and bigotry originate?
How are racism and bigotry passed on?
What can be done to begin fostering cooperation and understanding among people of diverse backgrounds?
Is there a difference between the way we treat recent immigrants to this country and citizens with nonEuropean backgrounds who immigrated several generations earlier? Why? Why not?

Scenario: WE DON'T WANT THEM

WHO

Billy—lives with his father. Billy is very loud in school and is somewhat of a leader. He sometimes decides to exclude others from playing in the kickball game at recess or other activities because he says they are "geeks", and others go along with his leadership.

Kendall and Jacob—live with their mother, who just relocated because of a new job. Kendall and Jacob are very uneasy about being in this strange and new place and wish that they hadn't moved.

WHAT

Kendall and Jacob came from a school where there was a large racial mix of students to this small New England town where there are very few African-Americans. In fact, Kendall and Jacob are the only African-Americans in their new school. It is recess, and Billy is telling Kendall and Jacob that they cannot join the games.

WHERE

On the playground at recess.

WHAT WOULD HAPPEN IF

a teacher found out what Billy was doing?
some of the other students decided to play with Kendall and Jacob anyway?
the students involved were all girls? a mixture of girls and boys?
the new students are from another ethnic background? another religion? a
different social class? a different perceived sexual orientation?

THINGS TO THINK ABOUT

Is Billy really racist, or does he just like the power he has with the other students? Can both be true?
Would things be different if other students stopped listening to Billy?
Where might Billy have gotten his negative ideas about people from backgrounds or cultures different from his own?

Scenario: THE SCHOOL BOARD MEETING

WHO

Carter—is in the 10th grade. He or she is involved in student government and tries to stay updated on current issues both at home and in the world. Carter is very perceptive and often comes up with good solutions to problems.

Aaron—is also in the 10th grade and is a friend of Carter's. Aaron has trouble in classes but tries hard. Unless an issue directly affects his or her life, Aaron rarely gets involved.

School board chairperson—runs a local insurance agency. He or she likes to avoid controversy because it helps the school run more smoothly and does not adversely affect his or her insurance business.

WHAT

The school board is considering the construction of a new middle school for the district at a public budget hearing in a few days. Only registered voters are allowed to speak at the meeting. Aaron and Carter feel that the voices of students are important and need to be heard and have approached the board chair about it.

WHERE

In the chair's business office.

WHAT WOULD HAPPEN IF

the chair tells them that they cannot speak?
the chair gives them time to speak; however, he or she makes stipulations on what they are allowed to say?
the chair doesn't feel that they need a middle school but the students do? vice versa?
the issue in question were the distribution of condoms at the local high school? some other issue?

THINGS TO THINK ABOUT

What issues in your town directly affect you? Why? Do you feel you have a say in what happens?
Is it important for students to be involved in the political issues around them?
Pick a "hot" issue in your town and discuss why it is important, how it affects you, and what you can do to make your opinions known.

Scenario: BUT HE'S GOT NO PLACE TO GO

WHO

Erin—is 15 years old. Erin and Mother live in a small city. Everyone likes Erin because he or she is exceptionally accepting and friendly.

Mother—is a single parent of an only child. Although the household consists of just the two of them, Mother still has a hard time making ends meet.

Sam—is 16 years old and hangs out with Erin. Sam and his or her parents have been homeless for several months. They got by during the warm weather, and Sam never told anyone at school. With winter coming, Sam's parents want to move some place warmer where they might find work. Sam doesn't want to leave and has confided in Erin.

WHAT

Sam has just told Erin what is going on. Erin decides to ask Mother if Sam can live with them.

WHERE

In the kitchen cleaning up the dinner dishes.

WHAT WOULD HAPPEN IF

Sam is present or is not present when Erin asks Mother?
Sam's mother were financially more secure?
Mother knows or doesn't know Sam's parents?
this were Sam's senior year in high school?
Sam and Erin were both boys? girls? a boy and a girl?

THINGS TO THINK ABOUT

Are there many homeless people in the town in which you live? How do you know?
What resources are available for homeless people in your area?
How can you tell if someone is homeless?
What can you do to help?
What causes people to become homeless?
Is homelessness mostly a social problem or a personal one? Could both be significant?

Scenario: THE INTERVIEW

WHO

Chris—is 16 years old and in the 10th grade. He or she has decided to get an after-school job.

Interviewer—is a person around 35 years of age and is manager of a local fast-food restaurant. The interviewer tends to be a bit rough on prospective employees.

WHAT

Chris applied for a job at the restaurant a week ago and today has an interview with the manager.

WHERE

In the dining room at the restaurant.

WHAT WOULD HAPPEN IF

Chris is extremely nervous and has a difficult time answering the questions?
Chris breezes through the questions with no problem?
the only question that Chris has a problem answering is, "What qualities do you have to contribute to this establishment?"
Chris is late for the interview?
the employer is in a very bad mood?

THINGS TO THINK ABOUT

How should you dress when applying for a job?
Is it a good idea to bring questions to ask the employer?
What kinds of questions are asked during an interview?
What are appropriate questions to be asked? Can the employer ask you about your family? Can he or she ask you about your age? drug usage? sexual orientation?

Note: This is a very useful scenario for most high school students, so we recommend giving as many students an opportunity to try it as possible. The class then can offer helpful feedback to the job applicants.

Scenario: THE SOUP KITCHEN

WHO

> Perry—is 17 years old and spends Monday nights helping in the soup kitchen at a local church.
>
> Reed—is 15 years old and has not helped in the kitchen before.

WHAT

> Reed thought that working at the soup kitchen would be very depressing. While serving the meal, Reed was surprised at how much everyone was smiling and at the diversity of people. The scene takes place as Perry and Reed are leaving.

WHERE

> Outside the church, about 8:00 at night.

WHAT WOULD HAPPEN IF

> Reed has a negative attitude about some of the people who were at the kitchen?
> Reed isn't sure how to react to some of the people with disabilities and asks Perry what to do?
> Reed is surprised how much he or she enjoyed working with the kitchen staff and wants to know how he or she can become a full-time volunteer?

THINGS TO THINK ABOUT

> How would you react to working with disabled persons?
> What other types of community services are there in your community?
> How does volunteering help your community? How does it help you?

Scenario: THE HUMANE SOCIETY

WHO

Chris—has been working at the Humane Society for a year. Chris enjoys working there because he or she loves animals.

Rat—is an older cat in the kennels. Chris named him "Rat" because, when Chris first arrived, this rare male calico looked like an overgrown rat. After only two weeks in the kennels, Rat's coat began to shine and he became a very playful animal. (This part should be played by a student who can voice what the animal might be feeling.)

Dr. Haskins—is the kennel's director.

Chris' parents—will not allow Chris to adopt a pet.

WHAT

Dr. Haskins pulled Chris aside yesterday because it is coming close to the time when Rat will be put to sleep. Dr. Haskins knows that Chris likes Rat and wants to give Chris time to find a home for the cat. Dr. Haskins offers to help Chris talk to his or her parents about adopting Rat. That night, Dr. Haskins drops by Chris's home with Rat in a traveling cage.

WHERE

In the kitchen after everyone gets home.

WHAT WOULD HAPPEN IF

Dr. Haskins allows Chris to hold Rat in front of his or her parents while telling them Rat's story and how well Chris has taken care of Rat?
after seeing Rat and Chris together, Chris's parents change their minds? don't change their minds?
Chris asks his or her parents to allow Rat to stay only until Chris can find a home for him?
the animal in question were a dog?

THINGS TO THINK ABOUT

How can we help unwanted animals?
How can we help prevent unwanted animals from being born?
How long can an animal shelter keep animals before having to destroy them?
How many unwanted animals does your local shelter serve each year? How many are adopted?

Chapter 10

DEATH/SUICIDE

List of Scenarios

- THE PILLS: Teen discovers a suicidal friend.
- FLUFFY'S GONE!: Child loses a pet.
- BE CAREFUL: A friend dies in a car accident.
- I SHOULD HAVE KNOWN: Teens react to suicide of a friend.
- WHAT SHOULD I DO?: Teen finds parent passed out from pills.
- IT'S NOT LOADED: A shooting accident.
- GOOD-BYE, GRANDPA: Death of a grandparent.
- IT'S MY FAULT: Death of a parent.
- HE OR SHE WAS THE BEST: Death of a teacher.
- WHERE'S TERRI?: A drowning at the class picnic.

RESOURCES

Most communities have affiliates of the State Department of Health and Human Services that serve children and youth (DYF, DCYS, etc.). Social workers at these or local mental health agencies in your area may have information on programs, brochures, or guest speakers that they could offer. If your community has a teen center, they may have resources that you could use. Religious and educational institutions, guidance counselors, and therapists often have programs, offer counseling, or both that can assist young people in these situations. Suicide prevention organizations, such as the Samaritans and local Hospice organizations, offer programs and often free counseling to individuals and groups to assist families and friends of those who commit suicide or die unexpectedly and to assist those who are suicidal.

Many schools also offer mediation programs, peer counseling programs, or both that you can recommend to members of your group. The National Association of Mediation Education (based in western Massachusetts, but with local and regional affiliates in many states) and the Re-Evaluation Counseling International Network (based in Seattle, WA, but with branches in every state and most Westernized countries) offer classes, school and community programs, and literature on these topics. Also, family therapy references can offer additional exercises and insights.

Scenario: THE PILLS

WHO

Jeremy—is an average kid and is not doing well in school right now. His parents are fighting all the time. He thinks they are going to get divorced and that it's his fault.

Amy—is a friend. Her parents were divorced several years ago.

WHAT

Amy walks in on Jeremy, who is concentrating on a handful of pills. She recognizes them as sleeping pills. Jeremy finally admits that things are going badly and that he wants to kill himself.

WHERE

Jeremy's bedroom.

WHAT WOULD HAPPEN IF

Jeremy had already taken the pills?
Instead of a problem at home, Jeremy has just had a fight with his girlfriend?

THINGS TO THINK ABOUT

Why do people commit suicide?
What should Amy do?
Where can Amy get help?
Should all suicidal threats be taken seriously?
What happens if someone is successful at their attempt at suicide?
What happens if someone attempts suicide but is not successful?
What happens to someone who is unsuccessful at suicide but has attempted it?
If you have had thoughts of killing yourself but never had intentions of going through with it, are you abnormal?
Do all people who try to commit suicide really want to die?
What are other options for dealing with intense negative feelings besides attempting suicide?
How do stressors such as divorce, illness, school failure, and being teased or harassed lead to suicidal feelings?

Scenario: FLUFFY'S GONE!

WHO

Pat—is any age and has had Fluffy since he or she was a small child. Pat is an only child and spent a lot of time alone with Fluffy.

J.J.—is Pat's best friend and is the same age as Pat. J.J. comes from a large family and was never allowed to have a pet. J.J. also spent a lot of time with Fluffy.

WHAT

Pat tells J.J. about finding Fluffy, dead of old age that morning. Pat is very sad. J.J. tries to comfort Pat and also feels very bad about Fluffy's death.

WHERE

At school during recess.

WHAT WOULD HAPPEN IF

Pat got another pet and named her Fluffy II?
They hold a funeral for Fluffy?
J.J. tells Pat that he or she is being stupid?

THINGS TO THINK ABOUT

How can J.J. comfort Pat if J.J. also is feeling sad?
Is it all right to grieve the loss of a pet?
How does one death remind us of other deaths or our own death?

Scenario: BE CAREFUL

WHO

Robin—is 16 years old and has just received a driver's license. Robin enjoys driving fast.

Rae and Toni—are also each 16. They are very good friends with Robin, but after the first time riding with Robin, they decided not to ride with Robin again.

WHAT

Robin was driving to school that day and was already an hour late. It was snowing very lightly. On the corner just before the school, there was a patch of ice lightly dusted with snow. Robin's car slid out of control and hit a big elm tree. Everyone in school heard the crash, but they did not find out what happened until it was announced over the intercom during second period. Toni and Rae are very upset. They ask for passes to the guidance office.

WHERE

Outside the guidance office.

WHAT WOULD HAPPEN IF

Robin was or was not seriously hurt?
Robin was killed on impact?
Toni is very upset but Rae acts as if he or she could care less? vice versa?
Toni and Rae were two males? two females? a male and a female?
the guidance counselor brings them into the office to talk about what happened?

THINGS TO THINK ABOUT

How can seatbelts and airbags prevent tragedy in accidents like this one?
How might this accident have been prevented?
What feelings might students experience upon hearing of the death or serious injury of a friend from a car accident?

Scenario: I SHOULD HAVE KNOWN

WHO

Jo—is in the eighth grade and has had the same best friend (Danny) since the first grade. When they got into junior high, they met B.J. and Dana. Now the four of them rarely are seen apart.

B.J.—is also in the eighth grade. Unlike Danny, B.J. has divorced parents. B.J. always talks to Danny about his or her own problems, but Danny rarely confides in B.J.

Dana—is an eighth grader like the others. Dana and Danny have a special relationship. They like daring each other to do things, such as walking across the ice on the river.

WHAT

Danny had not been in school that day. When Jo got home, his or her mother was waiting. Danny's father had called to tell Jo's mother that Danny had committed suicide. Jo is shocked. After a while, Jo calls the others and asks if they can meet right away.

WHERE

On the playground about 5:00 p.m.

WHAT WOULD HAPPEN IF

Danny had told one of the friends that he or she was contemplating suicide? Danny attempted suicide but did not succeed?

they don't find out until the next day at school when it is announced over the intercom?

the scene begins with Danny's telling his or her friend(s) that he or she is contemplating suicide?

THINGS TO THINK ABOUT

If someone tells you that he or she is contemplating suicide, what should you do?

If someone tells you that he or she is considering suicide, how can you determine the risk of whether or not they will actually do it?

If your friend tells you that he or she is going to commit suicide and you talk him or her out of it, should you still tell someone else? Why? Why not?

Scenario: WHAT SHOULD I DO?

WHO

J.T.—is any age. J.T.'s parents divorced three years ago. J.T. sees Father two or three times a month and lives with Mother. Things seemed fine up until last month. Now J.T. is becoming nervous because he or she doesn't know how to help Mother.

Mother—is a single parent. She lost her job last month and, after a few weeks, became very depressed. She rarely talks to J.T. anymore and spends her days sleeping.

WHAT

J.T. comes home from school and finds Mother on the floor with an empty pill bottle in her hand. J.T. tries to wake her, but she does not respond. J.T. notices that she is barely breathing and that her skin is very cold.

WHERE

The living room of their house.

WHAT WOULD HAPPEN IF

J.T. calls his or her father?
J.T. calls 911?
while J.T. is trying to decide what to do, he or she has to deal with a frightened younger sibling?
J.T. had brought a friend home after school?
J.T.'s mother is addicted to pain killers and J.T. has become accustomed to finding her passed out?
Mother is sitting there about to take the pills when J.T. arrives?

THINGS TO THINK ABOUT

What are the emergency numbers for your area?
What is the fastest way to get help to your home?
What can a young person do if they are concerned about a parent's behavior?

Scenario: IT'S NOT LOADED

WHO

Marty—is nine years old. Marty's parents work until 5:00 p.m., so Marty goes to Kendall's house until Marty's parents get home.

Kendall—is eight years old. Kendall likes to look at his or her father's gun collection. Kendall knows that the guns are off limits to touch, but it is okay to look at them.

Kendall's mother—usually allows the kids to play without being in eyesight but checks on them every once in a while.

WHAT

It is raining outside, so the two kids have been inside all day. Even though they have only been home from school an hour, they are bored. Kendall suggests that they go look at Father's gun collection. For some reason, the gun case had been left unlocked and the door is ajar. Kendall can't resist touching his or her favorite pistol and has to pick it up with two hands because it is heavy. (Assume that the gun is not loaded.)

WHERE

In the den.

WHAT WOULD HAPPEN IF

Marty wanted to hold the gun, too, and they started to fight over it?
Kendall and Marty decide to play cops and robbers with the gun?
Kendall's mother finds them playing with the gun?
they are able to look at the gun and put it back without anything happening or anyone finding out?
the gun were loaded?

THINGS TO THINK ABOUT

Should parents keep guns in the house?
What safety measures are necessary to avoid accidents with firearms?

Scenario: GOOD-BYE, GRANDPA

WHO

Stephe—is 11 years old. He or she loves to spend time with Grandfather, even though it is only possible a few times a year because he lives so far away.

Mother—is happy to send Stephe to Grandfather's house for a week or two during the summer, because Mother and Stephe get a break from each other. This summer Mother knows that Stephe will not be able to go because Grandpa is sick.

WHAT

Stephe and Mother are arguing because it is the end of summer and Stephe wants to go to Grandfather's even though he is sick. Stephe wants to be able to see Grandfather and maybe help take care of him. In the back of Stephe's mind is the thought that he or she wants to be able to say good-bye in case Grandfather dies. Mother wants to protect Stephe from seeing Grandfather sick so that Stephe can remember him the way he was.

WHERE

In the kitchen, washing and drying the dishes.

WHAT WOULD HAPPEN IF

Stephe's mother refuses to allow Stephe to visit Grandpa?
Stephe tells Mother how he or she feels about saying good-bye?
Grandpa comes to live with them for a few weeks until he has to go to the hospital?
Grandpa dies without being able to say good-bye to Stephe?
Stephe and Mother decide to go see Grandpa together?
Stephe and her grandfather were not very close and Stephe's mother wanted Stephe to visit but he or she did not want to?

THINGS TO THINK ABOUT

Should parents allow their children to visit ailing grandparents? Why? Why not?
Should parents allow their children to attend funerals? Why? Why not?
What are some ways that young people deal with the death of someone close?

Scenario: IT'S MY FAULT

WHO

Tory—is in the seventh grade. Tory is a fairly good student and is involved in sports. Right now, however, Tory has been challenging all the rules that his or her parents have set.

Casey—is in the fifth grade. He or she is very close to both his or her parents. Casey tries to be a "perfect child," but does not feel as if he or she succeeds.

Mother—is a professional mother. She has a part-time job as a seamstress while the kids are in school, but she basically schedules her life around her family.

WHAT

This morning before, Tory went to school, he or she had a fight with Father. On the way home from work, Father's car hit a patch of ice and ran into a tree. He was not wearing his seatbelt and was killed on impact. The scene begins with Mother telling Tory and Casey about the accident.

WHAT WOULD HAPPEN IF

Father is not killed but is critically injured?
their mother is not able to tell them because she is in shock? (It is a relative who tells Tory and Casey what happened.)
their mother tells them and then refuses to talk about it any further?

THINGS TO THINK ABOUT

If you were Tory, would you feel guilty? Is there a reason for Tory to feel guilty?
Should parents talk to their children about death and give children a chance to express how they feel?

Scenario: HE OR SHE WAS THE BEST

WHO

Jordy—is in the 10th grade. Like almost everyone else in the school, Jordy loves history class because the teacher, Ms. or Mr. Shaggnon ("Shaggs" as everyone called her or him), is one of the best teachers in the school.

Fern—is also in the 10th grade and in Shaggs' history class with Jordy.

Ms. or Mr. Schizmonio—the head of the history department. Ms. or Mr. Schizmonio sometimes takes over for absent teachers.

WHAT

When the two students walk into their history classroom, they instantly are disappointed because Ms. or Mr. Schizmonio is standing at the front of the classroom. That meant that Shaggs was absent today. After the bell rings and everyone is seated, Ms. or Mr. Schizmonio begins to tell the class that Ms. or Mr. Shaggnon had a heart attack the night before and had died. Ms. or Mr. Schizmonio allows the class period to be spent talking about how this affects the students.

WHERE

In Shaggs' history classroom.

WHAT WOULD HAPPEN IF

the students had been told over the intercom?
instead of a heart attack, the death was the result of an alcohol-related accident? a shooting?
there was someone in the class who was being unsupportive and cruel?
the school did not address the issue, and everyone found out about it from the newspapers?

THINGS TO THINK ABOUT

If a favorite teacher of yours died, how would you want your school to address the issue?

Note: This scenario also can be enacted by the whole group rather than just a few students. Alternatively, students may substitute in for Jordy and Fern as the scene progresses, to avoid confusion.

Scenario: WHERE'S TERRI?

WHO

The WHO in this scenario becomes the entire class. Choose one person to be Pat, the best friend of the classmate who drowned. Everyone else can play any characters they like. Students may choose to play characters very similar or very different from themselves.

WHAT

It is Monday. During the class picnic on Saturday, one of the students, Terri, drowned. The class members are trying to deal with their feelings.

WHERE

The classroom, before lessons have started.

WHAT WOULD HAPPEN IF

Pat felt responsible because he or she had encouraged Terri to go near the water?

one of the other classmates had a fight with Terri at the beginning of the picnic?

there had been horseplay that led to the accident?

there is a student in the class who was usually very cruel to Terri?

one or two of the students say that they don't care because they didn't like Terri anyway?

THINGS TO THINK ABOUT

What kind of impact may an event like this have on a group of students?
How can students protect each other from being hurt on school outings?

Note: If trying this scenario with the entire class becomes too confusing, select a small group to do the scene. Then allow other class members to substitute in so that anyone who has feelings or ideas to express has an opportunity to do so.

Chapter 11

VIOLENCE/ABUSE

List of Scenarios

- THE BABY-SITTER: A neglecting parent.
- I HATE YOU!: Baby-sitting for an abused child.
- I'M WARNING YOU: An older sibling physically abuses a younger sibling.
- HALLIE'S PROBLEM: Sexual abuse by an older brother.
- CHICKEN: Student conflict and violence.
- IT'S JUST FOR PROTECTION: Guns in school.
- DOMESTIC WARS: Dealing with parents fighting.
- "NO" MEANS "NO": Date rape.
- SHOULD I TELL?: Bad touches from a family member.
- I'M SORRY: Being in an abusive relationship.
- I CAN HELP YOU: Sexual harassment at work.
- YOU DON'T HAVE TO FAIL: Sexual harassment at school.

RESOURCES

Most communities have affiliates of the State Department of Health and Human Services that serve children and youth (DYF, DCYS, etc.). Social workers at these or local mental health agencies in your area may have information on programs, brochures, or guest speakers that they could offer. If your community has a teen center, they may have resources that you could use. Religious and educational institutions, guidance counselors, and therapists often have programs and/or offer counseling that can assist young people in these situations. Domestic violence agencies, crisis services, conflict resolution police specialists, sexual abuse and/or harassment prevention officials (some of whom are police, some of whom work in mental health agencies) can offer information and programs for violence and abuse prevention and recovery for survivors of abuse or violence.

Many schools also offer mediation programs, peer counseling programs, or both that you can recommend to members of your group. The National Association of Mediation Education (based in western Massachusetts, but with local and regional affiliates in many states) and the Re-Evaluation Counseling International Network (based in Seattle, WA, but with branches in every state and most Westernized countries) offer classes, school and community programs, and literature on these topics.

Scenario: THE BABY-SITTER

WHO

Mother—is in her late-20s and works days at the cafe earning minimum wage.

Saddie—is a teenaged baby-sitter and takes care of the baby when Mother is at work.

WHAT

The mother does not take proper care of the baby (e.g., properly feeding and bathing him or her, cleaning the apartment to create a safe environment, etc.). Saddie is concerned about the baby's health yet does not want to tell on the mother. Saddie decides to confront the mother instead.

WHERE

The apartment, one hour before mother has to leave for work.

WHAT WOULD HAPPEN IF

the mother does agree or does not agree to correct the situation?
the baby-sitter threatens to report the mother?
the baby-sitter quits?
the baby-sitter really needs the money from this job?

THINGS TO THINK ABOUT

Does the mother need to be reported? If so, to whom would the baby-sitter report her?
What is a safe environment for a baby?
What is proper care for a baby?
What is more important, proper care for the baby or protecting the mother by not telling on her?

Scenario: I HATE YOU!

WHO

Julia—is a high school student. She baby-sits Karen every day before and after Karen goes to school. Usually they get along, but lately Julia has had many problems with Karen's behavior.

Karen—a girl between 6 and 10 years of age. Karen really likes her baby-sitter, but she is feeling very angry right now because her father has been abusing her, sexually. Karen's mother refused to believe Karen, and they never talk about "it." Karen's parents are divorced, but Karen still has regular weekend visits with her father, who still abuses her.

WHAT

Karen gets angry with Julia and threatens to jump out the window or stab herself with a knife. Julia is very concerned. She realizes that something is wrong, but is not sure exactly what it is.

WHERE

Karen's living room.

WHAT WOULD HAPPEN IF

Julia is able to persuade Karen to tell her why she is so angry all the time?
Karen told Julia she was or is being sexually abused?
Karen is being physically abused by one or both parents?
the abuse has stopped, but whenever Karen gets into trouble, her mother brings up the situation and calls Karen a liar?

THINGS TO THINK ABOUT

What are some other reasons why Karen might be so angry?
What can Julia do to help Karen?
If you are aware that someone is being abused, what should you do?

Scenario: I'M WARNING YOU

WHO

Scott—is seven years old. He is just entering the first grade. He has an older sister and brother, and he doesn't get along very well with his sister. Scott is sick of getting picked on.

Sarah—is a very angry nine-year-old. She takes out her frustration on her younger brother, Scott. She believes things were fine before he was born. She blames him for the way their parents fight.

Brandon—is 10 years old. He has taken on the role of watching out for his younger siblings and tries to keep them from fighting.

WHAT

Sarah is angry. When she came in to watch TV, she took her shoes off. When Scott came in, he accidentally tripped on Sarah's shoes and fell, hitting Sarah in the leg. Sarah punched Scott in the nose. Brandon comes in to find Scott crying and bleeding and Sarah still angry.

WHERE

In the living room.

WHAT WOULD HAPPEN IF

Brandon is angry with Sarah and he tries to send her to her room, but she won't go?
Brandon threatens to call their father at work?
Scott asks Sarah why she is so mad at him?
Sarah walks away and leaves Brandon to comfort Scott?
their mother or father walks in during the fight?

THINGS TO THINK ABOUT

Should Brandon tell his parents what happened? Why? Why not?
How could Sarah learn to deal with her anger better?
Should Sarah be punished for her behavior?
Where could this family seek help to deal with their problems?

Scenario: HALLIE'S PROBLEM

WHO

Hallie—is 10 years old. She is a very timid and quiet girl. She has many problems with her mother, who has an alcohol problem and is verbally abusive to Hallie.

Hallie's mother—has an older son who is about 25 years old. She never wanted to have another child but was trying to save her marriage. However, Hallie's birth only made things worse and the husband left. The mother tries to ignore Hallie as much as possible.

WHAT

Hallie has just come home from her older brother's house and is very confused. The last two times that she has visited her brother, he touched her in places that made her very uncomfortable. She is frightened and tries to tell her mother.

WHERE

Hallie's home.

WHAT WOULD HAPPEN IF

Hallie's mother does believe her or does not believe her?
Hallie's mother does believe her but tells Hallie that it is her fault?
Hallie knows that her mother is not going to believe her, so she talks to another relative?
Hallie's brother has threatened to kill Hallie if she tells anyone what he has done?

THINGS TO THINK ABOUT

Is a victim ever responsible for having been abused?
If Hallie can't get her mother to believe her, should she give up or should she tell someone else?
Who else could Hallie talk to about this?
What will happen when Hallie finds someone who believes her?
Is it possible that Hallie's brother could hurt her for telling?
Would it be better for Hallie not to say anything?

Scenario: CHICKEN

WHO

Kimo—is in the eighth grade. He or she is usually a quiet person, but if pushed too far has a nasty temper. It is not very often that anyone will tangle with Kimo, but sometimes people just look for fights.

B.J.—is in the 10th grade. B.J. pushes Kimo in the halls all the time. B.J. thinks it is fun to push the younger kids around; for some reason it makes B.J. feel cool.

WHAT

B.J. has pushed Kimo in the halls more than once. Kimo finally has had it and decides to do something about what is happening. B.J. has been trying to arrange a fight after school. Kimo isn't sure what he or she wants to do.

WHERE

In the back parking lot.

WHAT WOULD HAPPEN IF

Kimo decides to fight? not to fight?
a teacher has seen B.J. push Kimo more than once and decides to step in?
B.J. and Kimo were two females? a male and a female?

THINGS TO THINK ABOUT

What are the consequences for fighting in your school?
What would be the consequences from your parents?
Are students looked down on by their peers if they back down from a fight?
What are some other ways to deal with a bully without fighting him or her?
Is it possible to transmit or contract the HIV virus during a fight? If so, how?

Scenario: IT'S JUST FOR PROTECTION

WHO

> Danny—is 13 years old and lives in a small suburb of a city. Danny lives with both parents but spends a lot of time at home alone.

> Vick—is the same age as Danny. Vick also has little supervision. They walk to school together.

WHAT

> Although they are not extremely prevalent, there are gangs in Danny and Vick's school. Sometimes when Danny and Vick are walking to school, a group of teens tries to pressure them into buying drugs. Sometimes they even push Danny and Vick around. Yesterday Danny told them that if they didn't bug off, then Danny was going to talk to the police. One of the gang members pulled out a gun and threatened to kill them if they said anything to anyone. The next day, when Vick and Danny were walking to school, Danny showed Vick the gun that he or she had taken from his or her dad's dresser.

WHERE

> On the corner by Danny's house.

WHAT WOULD HAPPEN IF

> Vick said that if Danny brought the gun to school, then Vick would not walk with Danny again?
> Vick thought the gun was a good idea?
> the school had just installed a metal detector at the front door and Danny was caught with the gun?
> the same bullies confront Danny and Vick while they have the gun?

THINGS TO THINK ABOUT

> Does your school have a gun or gang problem?
> What could a person in Danny's situation have done to protect himself or herself without using a weapon?
> What are the consequences for bringing in a weapon to school?

Scenario: DOMESTIC WARS

WHO

Tommy—is nine years old. Tommy shares a room with his little brother, Greg. At night, Tommy's parents often fight. Sometimes it is so bad that neither of the boys can sleep. Tommy tries to comfort Greg when he is scared.

Mr. or Ms. Jordon—is Tommy's third-grade teacher. He or she has sent home notes and had conferences with Tommy's parents regarding Tommy's often being tired in class and his problem concentrating on his work. The teacher suspects something may be wrong at home.

WHAT

Tommy does not know what to do. He is afraid to talk to anyone because his father has forbid him to tell anyone what goes on in the house. Last night was really bad, and both boys got very little sleep. Tommy made the decision to talk to his teacher at recess.

WHERE

In the classroom, during recess.

WHAT WOULD HAPPEN IF

Mr. or Ms. Jordon suggested that they call a conference with his mother? father? both parents?

Mr. or Ms. Jordon asked Tommy if he and his brother would like to talk to the school counselor?

Tommy asked Mr. or Ms. Jordon if he or she would not tell anyone else because he was afraid of what his father might do?

Tommy talked to a friend instead of a teacher?

THINGS TO THINK ABOUT

What are the options for dealing with a problem like this?

What are a teacher's legal responsibilities when a student relays information of this kind?

What are a friend's responsibilities when learning about this type of problem?

Scenario: "NO" MEANS "NO"

WHO

Karin—is 17 years old. She has had a steady boyfriend for three months.

Ann—is also 17 years old. She and Karin get along very well and tell each other everything.

Tammy—is a few months younger than the other two. She is a friend to both Karin and Ann but at times gets on their nerves.

WHAT

Karin's boyfriend came over last night when her parents were out. They had a few beers. Todd became bored with the movie and asked Karin if she wanted to go upstairs. Karin did not fully understand his intent but followed him. Todd started kissing her; then he unbuttoned her shirt. When Karin realized what was happening, she told him to stop, but he wouldn't. The next day, Ann and Tammy stop over after school to see why Karin was absent. Karin looks awful. After making them promise not to tell anyone, she tells the others what happened.

WHERE

In the living room.

WHAT WOULD HAPPEN IF

Ann is supportive of Karin, but Tammy thought that what happened was Karin's own fault?
Karin is not sure if Todd raped her or not?
Ann tells Karin that she should press charges against Todd?

THINGS TO THINK ABOUT

What situations constitute date rape?
What are some ways that young people can protect themselves from situations such as this?
Can guys be raped too? Can girls rape guys?
Where in your community can you get more information about rape and how to support someone who has been a victim?
What are your state's legal definitions of sexual assault? Of rape?

Scenario: SHOULD I TELL?

WHO

Gary—is 9 years old. He loves to spend time with his grandfather. They always have been good friends.

Gerry—is also 9 years old. He lives next door to Gary, and the two are close friends.

WHAT

Gary was with his grandfather last night, and his grandfather asked him to pull down his pants. His grandfather had never touched him like that before. Gary is confused. The next day, Gary tells Gerry what happened and asks whether or not he should tell anyone.

WHERE

On the playground at school, during recess.

WHAT WOULD HAPPEN IF

the characters were both girls? a girl and a boy?
before he tells Gerry, Gary makes him promise not to tell anyone about it?
Gerry tells Gary that he needs to tell a grown-up, but Gary refuses?
Gerry says that he will go with Gary if he will tell his mom or dad?
Gerry tells Gary that he cannot keep his promise to not tell anyone about this and insists that they tell a responsible adult.
the abusive relative is the grandmother?

THINGS TO THINK ABOUT

What is the difference between "good" and "bad" touches?
Where are the places on your body that no one else has the right to touch?
What could happen to Gary and his grandfather after Gary tells?
Why is it not good to hold information like this inside?
Is Gary in any way responsible for what his grandfather has done?

Scenario: I'M SORRY

WHO

Casey—is 19 years old. She is very much in love with Carey. Lately she has been treating him horribly.

Carey—loves Casey. It upsets him a lot that she takes all her anger out on him and pushes him around.

WHAT

Casey has been fighting with Carey constantly for months. She will get angry and ignore him, yell at him for no reason, and use sex as a way to get Carey to forgive her. Carey has decided to break up with Casey. Carey is having a very hard time dealing with this and feels that he is deserting her.

WHERE

In Carey's car.

WHAT WOULD HAPPEN IF

Casey apologizes and Carey forgives her?
Casey promises to get better if he doesn't leave?
Carey has been pushed so far to the edge that he doesn't believe anything Casey says?
Casey blames Carey for all the problems in their relationship?
Casey tells Carey that she had been sexually abused as a child and is having a lot of emotional problems right now?
this were a same-sex couple?
it were the male who was abusive toward the female?

THINGS TO THINK ABOUT

What are some warning signs of an abusive relationship?
Why do some people remain in an abusive relationship?
Where can a person get help to deal with this type of problem?
Are men or women more likely to be abusive in a relationship?
Are men or women more likely to be physically abusive in a relationship?

Scenario: I CAN HELP YOU

WHO

Mr. or Ms. Smith—is 28 years of age and is the assistant manager of Toys, the local toy store.

Fran—is 17 years old and has been working at Toys for about six months.

Jamie—is a co-worker of Fran's and is the same age.

WHAT

Mr. or Ms. Smith has been looking at Fran "a little weird" for a while. Although Fran feels uncomfortable, he or she isn't really sure if anything is really going on. There is another position opening at Toys that pays a little better. Fran is interested in the job and decides to go talk to Mr. or Ms. Smith about it. During the conversation, Mr. or Ms. Smith told Fran that he or she was sure that they could come to some arrangement. Mr. or Ms. Smith kissed Fran on the lips and then asked Fran to go out for dinner so that they could talk more about it. After Mr. or Ms. Smith left the room, Fran was upset and decided to talk to Jamie.

WHERE

In the coffee room at Toys.

WHAT WOULD HAPPEN IF

Jamie has had similar experiences with Mr. or Ms. Smith?
Jamie suggests that Fran talk to the manager of the store?
after talking with Jamie, Fran decides to confront Mr. or Ms. Smith alone? with Jamie present? with the store manager present?
Fran is considering going along with Mr. or Ms. Smith in order to get the promotion?

THINGS TO THINK ABOUT

What behavior is considered sexual harassment?
What steps can a person take when confronting or prosecuting someone who has been sexually harassing him or her?

Scenario: YOU DON'T HAVE TO FAIL

WHO

> Mr. or Ms. Dunkin—has been a teacher at the high school for several years and is generally liked by most students.

> Dana—is 15 years old and is in Mr. or Ms. Dunkin's English class. Dana has been having trouble with English this term and is concerned about failing.

WHAT

> Dana goes to see Mr. or Ms. Dunkin to inquire about the possibility of extra credit work to pull up his or her grade. Mr. or Ms. Dunkin tells Dana that there is an easier way to a better grade than doing extra credit assignments. Mr. or Ms. Dunkin goes to the door and locks it, then walks over to Dana and tries to kiss him or her.

WHERE

> In the classroom after school.

WHAT WOULD HAPPEN IF

> Dana tells Mr. or Ms. Dunkin to unlock the door, now, and the teacher listens? does not listen?
> Dana tells Mr. or Ms. Dunkin that he or she does not want to be seen as a possible date or sexual partner?
> Dana screams?
> Mr. or Ms. Dunkin is less aggressive in harassing Dana?

THINGS TO THINK ABOUT

> What are appropriate actions to take when a teacher or other authority figure behaves inappropriately?
> Who could you talk to if this happened to you?
> How can a situation such as this one be handled without increasing the potential danger to the student?
> Are there any situations in which an adult may approach a teen for sex? Why or why not?

Chapter 12

SEXUALITY/PREGNANCY/ RELATIONSHIPS

List of Scenarios

- UH, MOM . . . : Teen tells parent that she's pregnant.
- DO AS I SAY: Parents express sexual double standard.
- GROW UP: Pressure from friends to be sexually active.
- NOT MY CHILD: Parent confronts child about sexual activity.
- WE HAVE TO TALK: Teen tells boyfriend that she's pregnant.
- WE'RE RESPONSIBLE: Kids talk about condom distribution and use.
- IF YOU LOVE ME . . . : Pressure to have sex from a boyfriend or girlfriend.
- I DON'T KNOW HOW TO SAY THIS: Gay teen comes out to parents and/or friends.
- LET'S BE SAFE: Boyfriend and girlfriend talk about becoming sexually involved and safer sex.
- LOCKER ROOM TALK: Friends discuss their sexual experiences.
- WHAT DO I DO NOW?: Breaking up.

RESOURCES

Most communities have Planned Parenthood, Family Planning, Women's Health centers, abortion providers and options counselors, plus local hospitals or clinics that offer pregnancy testing, STD and HIV testing, and education.

Colleges and universities are especially well-equipped with hand-outs and infor-mation that you could tailor to your age group. In addition to those, check with your local or regional medical agencies for free treatment centers in your area and possible programs, brochures, or guest speakers that they could offer. Young parent groups, support groups for sexual identity questions, and programs for those leaving abusive relationships exist in most mental health and/or social service agencies. Many colleges and universities offer speakers on topics such as these, and many speak to groups for no charge.

There are also HIV/AIDS and lesbian/gay/bisexual/transgendered hotlines available in most calling areas: check with your 800 operator (1-800-555-1212). Some are especially established to serve young people, such as OUTRIGHT! Some are for parents, teachers, and/or friends of lesbian/gay/bisexual/transgen-dered people, such as P-FLAG.

Scenario: UH, MOM . . .

WHO

Mother—is in her early-30s. She supports herself and her daughter. Mother's ex-husband is often late with child support.

Jory—is 16 and pregnant. She doesn't know what to do. She's afraid to tell her mom, but her boyfriend, Darrin, insists that she do so. Darrin has told his parents already.

WHAT

Mother is in a bad mood already, but Jory promised Darrin that she would not wait any longer before telling Mother about the pregnancy.

WHERE

In the living room after dinner.

WHAT WOULD HAPPEN IF

Mother is understanding? angry?
Mother tells Jory to get an abortion?
Mother does or does not like Jory's boyfriend?
Jory decides to keep the baby?
Jory talks to her father?
Jory's boyfriend were there with her?
Mother had become pregnant at 16, just as Jory has?

THINGS TO THINK ABOUT

How would keeping the baby change Jory's life? her mother's life? the baby's father's life?
How might Jory feel about her mom encouraging her to have an abortion?
Whose responsibility is it to make the final decision?
What are Jory's options?

Scenario: DO AS I SAY

WHO

Mother—is in her late-30s. She works in an office as an accountant.

Father—is in his early-40s. He works in a bank.

Jasmine—is 18 years old. She is going into her first year of college.

John—is 16 years old. He is in the 11th grade.

WHAT

The family is talking about how teen boys and girls should act, and the parents express a double standard that views the issue of sexuality quite differently for their daughter than for their son.

WHERE

In the kitchen at dinner time.

WHAT WOULD HAPPEN IF

Mother sided with Jasmine, and father sided with John? vice versa?
Father agreed that the double standard was wrong and mother didn't? vice versa?
the son and daughter disagreed with their parents? each other?
Jasmine had been conceived before her parents were married?

THINGS TO THINK ABOUT

Is it appropriate to have a sexual double standard?
How might this double standard have originated? How is it perpetuated?
In what way might double-standard-thinking affect young men and women in today's society?
Should young people talk about sex with their parents?

Scenario: GROW UP

WHO

Lee—is 16 years old and has been dating Jory for three months. Lee is thinking about becoming sexually active but is not sure if he or she is ready.

Myn—is also 16 years old. Myn is Lee's best friend and has been sexually active for about a year.

WHAT

Lee has been discussing the situation with Myn for about two weeks. Every time the subject comes up, Myn tells Lee to stop being a baby. According to Myn, Lee should give in to the urges and live it up.

WHERE

In Myn's bedroom after school.

WHAT WOULD HAPPEN IF

Lee really isn't ready to take on the responsibility of sex but decides to follow Myn's advice anyway?
Lee decides that he or she is ready and plans a night with Jory?
Lee decides to postpone being sexually active for a while?
Lee is concerned that if he or she does not have sex with Jory that they might break up?

THINGS TO THINK ABOUT

How do you know when you are ready to become sexually active?
If you are planning to have a sexual experience with someone, what should you think about and be ready for?
Should friends pressure each other into being sexually active?
What is an intimate relationship like that does not include being sexually active? How do couples create closeness without having sex?

Scenario: NOT MY CHILD

WHO

Parent—always has tried to be involved in Ricky's life. They get along well and talk about almost everything.

Ricky—is 15 years old. Ricky talks to his or her parent about almost everything, but certain subjects are a little embarrassing.

WHAT

Ricky started dating Jacky about six months ago. Tonight Ricky's parent was emptying the trash from Ricky's room and found a used condom. When Ricky returned home from the movies, Parent confronted Ricky.

WHERE

In the living room.

WHAT WOULD HAPPEN IF

Ricky's parent did get upset? did not get upset?
Ricky tells Parent that what Ricky did was none of the Parent's business?
Parent wants to know with whom Ricky had sex?
Parent tells Ricky that he or she does not want Ricky around Jacky anymore?
Parent just wants to make sure that Ricky is well-informed about safer sex practices?
the characters in this scene were a mother and a daughter? a father and a son? a mother and a son? a father and a daughter? a grandparent and a grandchild?

THINGS TO THINK ABOUT

Should teens talk to their parents or other adults about being sexually active?
What are some ways you can keep yourself and your partner safe if you decide to become sexually active?

Scenario: WE HAVE TO TALK

WHO

Kimberly—is 17 years old. She and David have been dating for four or five months. There is even talk of an engagement. Kimberly wants to go to college when she graduates.

David—is 18 years old. He is in love with Kimberly but has high hopes for college.

WHAT

Kimberly and David have a sexual history together. They are usually very safe, but the last time they had intercourse, the condom slipped off. Kimberly missed her period and went to have a pregnancy test. The test came back positive, and now she has to tell David. Kimberly knows that David will want her to get an abortion, but she is not sure what she wants to do.

WHERE

Walking home from school.

WHAT WOULD HAPPEN IF

Kimberly and David are not sure what to do and decide to go talk to their parents?
David pressures Kimberly into getting an abortion?
David is or is not supportive?
Kimberly wants to get an abortion, but David wants her to have the baby?
Kimberly decides to have the baby but give it up for adoption?

THINGS TO THINK ABOUT

How would having a child at this age affect your life?
What would you do? Why?
How do you feel about abortion?
Who could Kimberly and David talk to if they decided not to tell their parents right away?

Scenario: WE'RE RESPONSIBLE

WHO

B.J.—is 17 years old. B.J. is very active in programs that promote safer sex practices and AIDS prevention. B.J. often can be found talking with and educating peers.

Chris—also is 17 years old. Chris has been sexually active in the past and tries to stay very educated about STDs.

Pat—also is 17 years old. Pat has decided to postpone sexual intercourse until after marriage.

WHAT

Some of the parents in the school district have started to discuss condom distribution in the school. B.J.'s advisor asked him or her to take a survey of students' thoughts on the issue, then give a speech to the PTO telling what he or she discovered. Chris and Pat are having lunch together when B.J. arrives.

WHERE

In the school cafeteria.

WHAT WOULD HAPPEN IF

Chris supports condom distribution in the school and Pat does not? vice versa?
B.J. found that most students interviewed on the issue do or do not want condom distribution in the school?
the characters are all boys? all girls? a combination?

THINGS TO THINK ABOUT

Is condom distribution appropriate and necessary in a school environment?
Who should make this decision? parents? students? school administration?
Why do you think condom distribution is such a hot issue?

Scenario: IF YOU LOVE ME . . .

WHO

> Sandy—is 15 years old. She has been dating Danny for about a month. Sandy has made the decision to postpone sexual intercourse.

> Danny—is 16 years old. Danny has been trying to persuade Sandy to have sex with him.

WHAT

> Danny has decided that if Sandy does not consent to have sex with him, he will break up with her. Sandy still wants to postpone having sex, but she also does not want Danny to break up with her.

WHERE

> On Sandy's back porch while her parents are out.

WHAT WOULD HAPPEN IF

> Sandy does or does not give in to the pressure?
> it were Sandy who is pressuring Danny?
> Sandy's mother or father overhears their conversation?
> Sandy and Danny are a gay or lesbian couple?

THINGS TO THINK ABOUT

> How can you tell when you are ready to have a sexual relationship with someone?
> Is pressuring someone to have sex a type of sexual harassment?

Scenario: I DON'T KNOW HOW TO SAY THIS

WHO

Lee—is 17 years old, is very outgoing, and generally is involved in many activities. Lately Lee has been coming to terms with the fact he or she is gay but has yet to share this information with anyone.

Parents—both work full-time. Mom is a physics professor, and Dad is a teacher at a middle school. Both are fairly accepting of other lifestyles but do believe that Lee's behavior reflects on their family.

WHAT

Lee's parents have noticed that Lee does not date. They believe that the situation is due either to the fact that Lee is shy or to the fact that he or she just doesn't have time to date. This weekend they are planning a dinner party and suggest that Lee invite Jamie, the teenage child of a friend. Lee decides that it is time to tell his or her parents that he or she is homosexual.

WHERE

In the living room after the party.

WHAT WOULD HAPPEN IF

Lee's parents do or do not accept this information?
Mom accepts it but Dad doesn't? vice versa?
Lee were telling his or her best friend? a group of friends?
Lee lives in an alternate universe where it is the norm to be homosexual, and he or she has to tell his or her parents that he or she is heterosexual?

Note: The "alternate universe" scene is a good way to look at the issue of homosexuality without allowing students to put down others because of sexual orientation or to fall into stereotypical behaviors.

THINGS TO THINK ABOUT

In what ways is it safe or unsafe for a gay youth to come out in your school or community?
Is sexual orientation a matter of either-or, or does it exist on a continuum?
In what ways does our culture create and perpetuate homophobic attitudes?

Scenario: LET'S BE SAFE

WHO

Jay—is 17 years old. He has been dating Lana for about four months.

Lana—also is 17 years old. She has dated quite a few guys in the past couple of years but has had very few serious relationships. Lana is nervous because her relationship with Jay seems to be heading in that direction.

WHAT

Lana wants to bring up the subject of becoming sexually active and of following safer sexual practices. She wants to find out how Jay feels about it but is very nervous about approaching him. What she doesn't know is that Jay is having the same thoughts. Today, Lana decided that the best way to talk about it was just to say what she was thinking. She plans to talk to Jay after school.

WHERE

In Jay's room.

WHAT WOULD HAPPEN IF

it were Jay bringing up the subject and not Lana?
Jay is ready to take on sexual responsibilities, but Lana is not? vice versa?
they both decide to become sexually active with each other, but one does
   not want to use condoms?
this were a gay or lesbian couple?

THINGS TO THINK ABOUT

If you cannot talk to your partner about sex, do you feel that you are ready
   as a couple to take on that responsibility?
Whose responsibility is it to bring up the subject of safer sexual habits?
Do most young people make a conscious and mutual decision to have
   intercourse, or does it just happen?
Can a couple decide to become sexually active and still decide to postpone
   intercourse?
What does it mean to be sexual with another person?

Scenario: LOCKER ROOM TALK

This scenario is designed to offer a comparison between the ways in which some young men and some young women talk about sex. Two scenes are set up, side by side, and the action switches back and forth between them.

WHO

In each group we suggest three teens. One is sexually active already. One has decided to postpone sexual intercourse. One is uncertain about the choice.

WHAT

The friends are engaged in a conversation about weekend plans and a party at which there will be no parents or chaperons. The talk turns to sex.

WHERE

The locker room.

WHAT WOULD HAPPEN IF

all the friends were or were not already sexually active?
all the friends were 13? 15? 17?
the conversation begins when one friend is boasting about a sexual conquest?

THINGS TO THINK ABOUT

Do young men and women have different points of view on being sexually active?
Do young women talk about sex differently from young men?
If you feel there is a difference, what might account for it?

Scenario: WHAT DO I DO NOW?

WHO

Jamie—is a girl between 17 and 19 years old. She has known and loved Jordon for three years. She feels that she is very lucky to have him.

Jordon—is a guy about the same age as Jamie. He loves Jamie very much. Jordan's family is moving 500 miles away, and he is having problems figuring out how to tell Jamie.

WHAT

Jamie and Jordon are celebrating their anniversary with dinner at a nice restaurant. Jamie tells him that she hopes they can be together forever. Jordan decides it is unfair to wait any longer to tell Jamie about the move.

WHERE

A moderately priced restaurant, during dinner.

WHAT WOULD HAPPEN IF

they decide to break up?
Jordon asks Jamie to marry him? she says yes? she says no?
Jamie is the one who is moving away?
Jordon or Jamie is not moving but wants to date someone else?

THINGS TO THINK ABOUT

Is it possible to maintain a long-distance relationship?
How do you know when you are ready to be married?
Is there a best way to break up?

PART C
GENERAL REFERENCES
AND
RESOURCES

REFERENCES & RESOURCES

The following is a list of references and resources that may be useful.

Blatner, A. (1973). *Acting in: Practical applications of psychodramatic methods in everyday life*. New York: Springer.

Blatner, A., & Blatner, A. (1988). *Foundations of psychodrama: History, theory, and practice* (3rd ed.). New York: Springer.

Boal, A. (1992). *Games for actors and non-actors*. Routledge, NY: Routledge.

Dayton, T. (1990). *Drama games*. New York: Innerlook.

Johnstone, K. (1987). *Improv: Improvisation and the theatre*. Routledge, NY: Routledge.

Spolin, V. (1975). *Theatre game file*. St. Louis, MO: Cemrel.

Spolin, V. (1985a). *Improvisations for the theatre*. Evanston, IL: Northwestern University.

Spolin, V. (1985b). *Theater games for rehearsal: A director's handbook*. Evanston, IL: Northwestern University.

Sturkie, J., & Cassady, M. (1990). *Acting it out*. San Jose, CA: Resource Publications.

ABOUT THE AUTHORS

Mario Cossa, MA, RDT, CP, is the creator and Program Director of ACTING OUT. ACTING OUT evolved from Cossa's 20 years of experience working professionally in theatre and teaching theatre arts to children and adolescents. Cossa is also an adjunct faculty member at Antioch/New England Graduate School, where he teaches Advanced Group Psychotherapy: Action Methods; and Introduction to Psychodrama.

Sally S. Fleischmann Ember, M.Ed., holds advanced degrees in Teacher Education and Curriculum Reform, focusing on multicultural education and inter-disciplinary curricula. In addition to being Educational Coordinator for ACTING OUT, Ember teaches adolescents and young adults in a variety of disciplines and often uses theatre in her courses. Ember's son, Merlyn, was born in 1980; they live in Keene, NH.

Lauren (Glass) Grover was a founding member of ACTING OUT in her junior year of high school. She helped with development of many of the scenes in this book and is very proud to have been a part of such an important process for so many people. She is married to Martin Grover, also a former AO member, and works as a radio personality in Concord, NH.

Jennifer L. (Russell) Hazelwood, AS, was a member of the first ACTING OUT group. For eight years, she has been an AO member, office staffer, or performer. Now a leader-in-training with AO, she has been a co-leader of a sixth-grade group. With an Associates degree in Elementary Education and Spanish, Hazelwood is pursuing a Bachelor's degree. The mother of a one-year-old, Hazelwood recently was married to another AO participant.